MISHANDLED:

SETTING THE RECORD STRAIGHT ON FREQUENTLY ABUSED BIBLE VERSES

BY

JOHN MACARTHUR

SCAN **THIS CODE** WITH YOUR SMARTPHONE
OR OTHER DEVICE TO FOLLOW
ALONG WITH THE SERMON AUDIO.

ISBN:978-1-955292-12-2

Printed in the United States of America

Valencia, California

CONTENTS

A B U S I N G

T H E   P O O R

I N T R O D U C T I O N

"And He looked up and saw the rich putting their gifts into the treasury. And He saw a poor widow putting in two small copper coins. And He said, 'Truly I say to you, this poor widow put in more than all of them; for they all out of their surplus put into the offering; but she out of her poverty put in all that she had to live on'" (Luke 21:1–4).

The account of the widow's mites is a very familiar portion of Scripture. If you're thinking to yourself, "Here comes another lesson on sacrificial giving," you might be justified because that is how this passage is universally taught. We are always told to give the way this widow gave. But let's back up and reexamine the text as well as the *context*, so we can interpret it all correctly.

A. A Fateful Day

It was Wednesday of Passion Week, the final week of our Lord's life. Jesus had entered Jerusalem on Monday, cleansed the Temple on Tuesday, and now, on Wednesday, He taught the multitudes in the Temple courtyard all day.

1. Silencing the religious leaders

On this Wednesday, the false religious leaders of Judaism had been testing Jesus with questions, trying to trap Him in His words so they might have grounds for a death sentence. But Jesus silenced them with His answer every time, thwarting their schemes and forcing them to fabricate a reason for the Romans to execute Him on Friday. They had no more questions to ask.

2. Ignoring the crowd

After a long day of teaching, Jesus no longer addressed the crowd. They had shown themselves to be fickle. The people may have hailed Him as Messiah when He entered Jerusalem, but they would cry out for His blood mere days later.

3. Judging Israel's rejection

In fact, if you follow the flow of the text from

Luke 21:5, you can see the theme of this section is judgment. The ministry of our Lord in these three years had come to its end. There were no more gospel invitations or clarifications to the crowds and leaders. Jesus had finished with them. Their final assessment was that He was not the Messiah they wanted, and they rejected Him—both the religious leaders and common people.

So verse 5 begins a long message of judgment. This judgment was to come in AD 70 with the destruction of the Temple, the city of Jerusalem, and the nation Israel, and would last until the return of Jesus—these two thousand years and beyond.

Even Jesus' warning at the end of Luke 20 is clearly a word of judgment: "Beware of the scribes" (vv. 46–47). While Luke only gives a couple of verses containing our Lord's warnings against the scribes and the Pharisees, Matthew 23:1–39 gives a full account of His censure. There He pronounced judgment on the leaders and therefore judgment on the nation who followed them in rejecting Christ.

B. A Foreboding Setting

Situated in between Jesus' condemnations—the one directed at the leaders, the other at the entire religious system and nation—is this vignette about a widow dropping two copper pennies into the

Temple's offering receptacle. Why did Jesus inject this moment of reflection upon the widow's offering after a diatribe against religious hypocrites and before a pronunciation of enduring judgment? Why is this here?

LESSON

I. THE WIDOW AND GIVING

Universally, commentators tell us that this account gives us a glimpse of true worship against the backdrop of the false worship that dominated the Temple. It is a beautiful little story in the midst of ugliness, they say, a light in the midst of darkness. It is an illustration of giving as a sincere act of worship contrasted with the spiritual leaders' pride and self-righteousness.

A. The Interpretations Proposed

While scholars agree that this passage is a lesson on giving, they can't agree *what* the lesson is. If you were to survey commentaries on this passage, you would find many different suggestions, and few in agreement. For example:

1. The residual—Some say Jesus is teaching that the measure of a gift is not how much you give but what you have left afterward.

2. The sacrifice—Another option is that the true measure of a gift is the amount of self-denial involved. What does it cost the individual? This is similar to the previous suggestion, but the emphasis is on the sacrifice the giver makes. This widow gave everything that she had, so it's about the percentage you give of your livelihood.

3. The attitude—A third related possibility is that the true measure of a gift is the attitude with which you give it. Is the giver selfless and humble? Is it an act of surrender? Is the giver expressing love for God, devotion to God, trust in God?

4. The impoverishment—A fourth suggestion is that the gift that truly pleases God is giving everything and taking a vow of poverty.

B. The Interpretations Disproved

Virtually everyone who writes on this text defends one or some combination of the above views. But none of them adequately explains the passage. In fact, they don't actually make sense—worse, they appear to be imposed on the text rather than drawn from it. Why do I say that? Because Jesus never made *any* of those points about the widow's gift.

1. Jesus' silence

a. Concerning the gift

He did not teach anything about:

       1) How much ought to remain after the gift

       2) How much it should cost the giver

       3) The attitude of the giver

       4) Taking a vow of poverty

   b. Concerning the rich

       Furthermore, Jesus didn't rebuke the rich people's giving by saying:

       1) They had too much left over

       2) Their gifts weren't costly enough

       3) They had a bad attitude

       4) They should have given everything

   c. Concerning the widow

       In fact, Jesus did not even commend the widow's giving. He did not say:

       1) She had the right amount left over

       2) It cost her the right amount

       3) She had a good attitude

       4) She was right to give everything

2. Jesus' statement

   Jesus only said the following about the widow's gift: She gave more than everyone else because she gave everything she had.

3. Jesus' point

Jesus did not comment on whether the widow or the rich people should or shouldn't have given, or why, or with what attitude. The widow's outward action is all you see. We don't know her motive because the Lord did not draw any conclusions or develop any principles or otherwise define the situation. And that's because those have nothing to do with the point of this story.

If Jesus had intended to teach a lesson on giving, He would have at least hinted at what that lesson is. But He didn't. Therefore, we must conclude that this account is not a lesson on giving.

4. Jesus' expectation

The one inarguable fact is that the widow gave everything. So if there were one lesson so obvious it didn't need to be stated, it would be that God expects you to give 100 percent of what you have.

But that is ridiculous, irresponsible, and foolish. In fact, it is contrary to Scripture, which is clear that God does not expect you to impoverish yourself by giving all that you have.

5. Jesus' concern

Another factor that militates against these interpretations is the context. Why would Jesus insert a little lesson on giving at such a pivotal and somber moment? Jesus is occupied with the coming judgment on the false religious establishment.

The context before and after this passage concerns the approaching condemnation of wicked spiritual leaders and their corrupt religious system. Luke wrote, "And while some were talking about the temple, that it was adorned with beautiful stones and votive gifts, He said, 'As for these things which you are looking at, the days will come in which there will not be left one stone upon another which will not be torn down'" (Luke 21:5–6).

This vignette is in between a diatribe against false religious leaders (Luke 20:46–47; cf. Matt. 23:1–39) and a pronouncement of judgment on their religious system (Luke 21:5–36).

II. THE WIDOW AND RELIGIOUS EXPLOITATION

So if it isn't about giving, what exactly is this story about?

A. A Clear Message

This account is not obscure. It is not one of those passages of Scripture that is especially profound, nor does it have some kind of deep, hidden meaning. It is not a particularly complex passage. It is simple and clear.

The bottom line is this: Jesus saw a widow give more than everybody else. Her involvement in religion cost her more than anybody else because it cost her everything. And that was obvious enough—the disciples understood without seeking clarification.

B. A Gift Without Commendation

It's a major assumption to interpret this widow as a model for Christian giving—that assumes that Jesus was pleased with what she did. But Jesus gave no indication of that. In fact, I think the widow's actions displeased Jesus; I think the whole incident angered Him.

C. A Religion of Corruption

1. Infuriating extortion

As a person who loves the Lord and cares for people, how would you feel if you saw a destitute widow give her only possessions to a religious system? You would condemn that system. The thought of an impoverished woman giving up her last hope of life to religion is sickening. This woman had been woefully victimized by a repulsive religious system. Any religion that is built on the backs of the poor is a corrupt, false religion. It's tragic, painful, and angering. And that's how Jesus saw it.

2. Blessing for sale

> The Jewish rabbis taught that salvation was purchased with alms. This desperate widow, hoping that she might be able to buy some kind of blessing or relief for herself, dutifully threw her last two coins into the treasury. But God does not want a widow to give up her last two cents—no passage in the Bible teaches such a thing.

MODERN-DAY PHARISEES

A contemporary equivalent to this kind of fraud exists within the Charismatic church today. It is commonly called "seed faith." The concept of a seed faith offering is that those who give to the Lord's work (which is usually the ministry of a wealthy prosperity preacher) can expect to receive a much larger sum of money back from the Lord. "Sow a seed of faith [i.e. give a financial gift] and see the Lord produce a hundredfold," they say. The charlatans who appeal for these offerings have no concern for those who are poor or in debt. In fact, they tell those people that their circumstances are just an opportunity for them to give with more faith and thus receive more back from the Lord. Such hucksters victimize the poor with false promises and rob them of the little they have.

3. Overwhelming hypocrisy

   a. Transgressing the commandment

   In Matthew 15 the Pharisees and scribes were confronting Jesus because the disciples didn't perform the ceremonial washings that the Jewish religious leaders had invented. "'Why do Your disciples break the tradition of the elders? For they do not wash their hands when they eat bread.' And He answered and said to them, 'Why do you yourselves transgress the commandment of God for the sake of your tradition?'" (vv. 2–3). The Jews had created a false religious system in the name of God which transgressed the commandment of God.

   b. Invalidating God's Word

   Jesus gave the perfect illustration of their hypocrisy in verses 4–6: "God said, 'Honor your father and mother,' and, 'He who speaks evil of father or mother is to be put to death.' But you say, 'Whoever says to his father or mother, "Whatever I have that would help you has been given to God," he is not to honor his father or his mother.' And by this you invalidated the word of God for the sake of your tradition."

   The law of God commanded the Jews to honor their father and mother (cf. Ex. 20:12; Deut. 5:16), and that included ensuring that their needs were met. But in order to evade that requirement, and to purchase and parade their righteousness, they would tell their parents that they were giving to God instead—and willingly leave their mother and father destitute. Rather than giving to the needy, as God's law required, they made a tradition of violating His law by neglecting the needy to give that money to Him. Matthew 15:9 reads, "In vain do they worship Me, teaching as doctrines the precepts of men."

The Ten Commandments gave children the responsibility to help their parents when they need care and provision because God is concerned that people's needs are met. To neglect that responsibility, even because you gave the money to God, is to violate the law of God with your tradition.

c. Sanctioning the unlawful

The parallel account in Mark 7:8–13 emphasizes the same hypocrisy in the religious leaders. Jesus said to the Pharisees and scribes, "'Neglecting the commandment of God, you hold to the tradition of men.' He was also saying to them, 'You are experts at setting aside the commandment of God in order to keep your tradition. For Moses said, "Honor your father and your mother"; and, "He who speaks evil of father or mother, is to be put to death"; but you say, "If a man says to his father or his mother, whatever I have that would help you is Corban (that is to say, given to God)," you no longer permit him to do anything for his father or his mother; thus invalidating the word of God by your tradition which you have handed down; and you do many things such as that.'"

The religious leaders had a name for this kind of gift: Corban, which means "devoted to God." All they had to do was say that the money was "Corban," and they were cleared of the responsibility to give it to their family. Thus, they customarily invalidated the word of God with their man-made religion.

d. Missing the priority

Judaism had developed into a system that abused poor people. These passages demonstrate that God's priority is meeting basic human needs before giving religious offerings. God's law was not given to impoverish people, but to help them. To adapt a phrase from Jesus, man was not made for the law, but the law was made for man.

So we can conclude that this woman was part of a system that took the last two cents out of her hand on the pretense that her offering was necessary to please God. She was manipulated and made destitute by a corrupt religious system she was trying to live up to, in order to earn heaven.

D. A Downcast Teacher (v. 1*a*)

"And He [Jesus] looked up . . ."

1. His position

The opening statement of Luke 21:1 assumes that Jesus was first looking down. The parallel verse, Mark 12:41, says that He was sitting down opposite the treasury. Luke 20:46–47 briefly includes Jesus' damning statements about the scribes. This weighty speech, which occupies 39 verses in Matthew 23, certainly gave Jesus a reason to sit and look down in sober reflection.

2. His rejection

Jesus is at the end of a full day of teaching and debating in the midst of massive crowds who jostled to listen to Him. That alone would have been physically exhausting, but there was also the emotion of the damnation speech of Matthew 23. This was a very low moment of Jesus' life, perhaps the lowest thus far. After all the years of ministry—the sermons preached, the questions answered, the miracles done—it all came down to Israel's religious leaders rejecting Him with the nation's backing.

3. His denunciation

Jesus gave this blistering malediction against the false religious leaders, using the word "woe" to designate them as cursed, damned, consigned to judgment (Matt. 23:13, 14, 15, 16, 23, 25, 27, 29). He calls them "hypocrites" (vv. 13, 14, 15, 23, 25, 27, 29), "blind guides" (vv. 16, 24), "fools and blind men" (v. 17), and blind Pharisees (v. 26). He repeatedly pronounces, "Woe to you, scribes and Pharisees, hypocrites!" (vv. 13, 14, 15, 23, 25, 27, 29).

4. His last word

This declaration of damnation ends with verses 37–38, "Jerusalem, Jerusalem, who kills the prophets and stones those who are sent to her! How often I wanted to gather your children together, the way a hen gathers her chicks under her wings, and you were unwilling. Behold, your house is being left to you desolate!" It was over; they faced unrelenting judgment until they could say, "Blessed is He who comes in the name of the Lord!" (v. 39)—until Christ's return. This is a sad final message. It was Jesus' final message, and it was devastating—not only to the leaders and the nation, but also to the Lord Himself.

5. His devastation

Jesus wasn't dealing with physical weariness alone. He was also facing the agonizing reality of the sinful rebellion and unbelief of Israel. He shed tears when He walked into the city (Luke 19:41), and He was still weeping in chapter 21. He had just proclaimed the heart-wrenching prophecy of judgment, and now He sat, looking down, burdened by the damning religion of Judaism. John 1:10–11, "He was in the world, and the world was made through Him, and the world did not know Him. He came to His own, and those who were His own did not receive Him."

E. An Ostentatious Tradition (v. 1*b*)

". . . and [He] saw the rich putting their gifts into the treasury."

1. The show

Jesus had said in Matthew 6 that giving ought to be done in secret. But the Jewish religious system had developed a deliberately public way to do it: Pharisees would arrange for trumpets to sound when they arrived at the Temple to give (Matt. 6:2). Thus, the givers' generosity was put on display for all to see, and on this occasion, Jesus was the one who noticed them putting money in the Temple treasury.

2. The arena

The court Jesus sat in was a large, open part of the Temple area called the Court of the Women. There was an inner court only men could enter, but Jesus taught in the Court of the Women so that everyone could come and hear Him.

Luke calls it "the treasury" because the religious leaders had designed a place in this court for the people to give their monetary offerings. They set up thirteen shofars—hollowed and polished ram's horns—into which people dropped their money. Each horn was labeled for a different fund so the givers knew what the money would go toward: old shekel dues, new shekel dues, bird offerings, wood, incense, gold, free will, and so on. People would approach this very public area and openly showcase their giving by dropping their money into these shofars.

"Treasury" (Gk., *gazophulakion*) comes from two words: *gaza*, meaning "treasury," and *phulakē* meaning "guard" or "prison." This is ironically reflective of what was happening with the Temple treasury: Once people threw their money in, it was kept securely in there—it certainly wasn't coming back out to the benefit of the givers.

THE HEARTBEAT OF HERETICS

To this day, the treasury is the real center of false religion.

Peter said that false teachers exploit people in greed (2 Pet. 2:3) and that their hearts are trained in greed (v. 14). They "[love] the wages of unrighteousness" (v. 15). Paul wrote that religious conmen teach falsehoods for the sake of "sordid gain" (Titus 1:11) and use godliness as a way to acquire cash (1 Tim. 6:5).

The Jewish religious leaders fit those descriptions. Luke 16:14 describes the Pharisees as "lovers of money." The Sadducees, who ran the Temple franchises, were also lovers of money, as shown by Jesus' words against them: "'My house shall be a house of prayer,' but you have made it a robbers' den" (Luke 19:46). They used the Temple grounds to swindle people with sales of sacrificial animals and coin exchange. As Scripture warns us, "the love of money is a root of all sorts of evil" (1 Tim. 6:10). It is a certain mark of false religion.

---

3. The bounty

So Jesus observed the normal course of false religion, deceiving souls with the empty promise of blessing and salvation in exchange for money. The "rich" people of verse 1 are referred to as *plousios* in the Greek text, which means they had a full supply. They weren't necessarily the wealthiest people in Israel, but they had plenty to live on and could give generous offerings and still have a decent surplus (see also Mark 12:41).

F. A Donation to the Coffer (vv. 2–4)

This religious system demanded money to prosper the men at the top. That's what false religion always does—it was the pattern then, and it is still the pattern now. And so Jesus watched the people in this open court, dutifully following the demands of their religious leaders in self-righteous acts of giving to buy favor from God.

"And He saw a poor widow putting in two small copper coins. And He said, 'Truly I say to you, this poor widow put in more than all of them; for they all out of their surplus put into the offering; but she out of her poverty put in all that she had to live on.'"

1. A poor widow

For the most part, Israel was prosperous, and many people could afford to make these kinds of donations. But the Lord spotted one widow (v. 2), and the text calls her "poor" (Gk., *penichran*), meaning she was needy but not destitute. She had very little but was not at the bottom yet. And she was putting two "small copper coins" (Gk., *lepta*), the smallest coins in their currency, into the receptacle.

2. A despised widow

Only a few verses before our passage, Jesus told His disciples, "Beware of the scribes, who like to walk around in long robes, and love respectful greetings in the market places, and chief seats in the synagogues and places of honor at banquets, *who devour widows' houses*" (Luke 20:46–47, emphasis added). That is, they built their financial success on the backs of widows.

The Pharisees, Sadducees, and scribes disdained widows as being under God's judgment. They presumed every widow was poor and defenseless because God was punishing her, and that they as leaders should aid God by making life difficult for her. Furthermore, widows were women, and women were second-class in their eyes. In fact, Pharisees would daily pray, "Lord, make me not a Gentile or a woman." Widows were easy prey for the false religious system.

3. An exploited widow

The connection between our passage and the preceding verses is abundantly clear. Jesus and His disciples were seeing a real-life example of one of the abused widows Jesus had just described. She was being devoured by a religious system as she gave her last two coins in an attempt to live up to that system's demands.

Again, there is no comment on whether she gave out of desperation or devotion, legalism or love. The Lord did not commend her or make her an example or validate what she did. There is nothing in this passage to say that it pleased Him. Instead, Jesus said that this gift cost the widow more than everyone else (v. 3).

The more needy widows became, the more desperate they became, the more they thought they needed to buy God's blessing. They were belittled as objects of God's punishment, relegated to second-class citizens, and exploited. Thus, the religious leaders took advantage of this widow and lined their pockets with "all that she had to live on" (v. 4). Now that they had taken everything from her, she would go home and die.

4. A forsaken widow

Scripture repeatedly teaches God's people to take care of widows (e.g., Ex. 22:22; Deut. 10:18–19; 14:28–29; 24:19–21; 26:12–13; 27:19; Isa. 1:17; Jer. 22:3; Zech. 7:9–10; Mal. 3:5; Acts 6:1–3; 1 Tim. 5:3–16; Jas. 1:27). Not only are there prohibitions against mistreating them, there are also many commands instructing believers to supply their needs.

The real tragedy that struck our Lord here was that the religious leaders forsook their duty and perpetrated their abuse—and all in the name of God and in the house of God. They had turned the Temple into a den of robbers who stooped so low as to bankrupt those who had the least.

5. A destitute widow

Verse 2 called this widow "poor" (Gk., *penichros*), which means she was needy. But in verse 3 Jesus calls her *ptōchos*, meaning she was destitute. She regressed to a new level of poverty because she gave up her last two coins. She had handed over everything she had to a false religious system.

G. A Shocking Conclusion (vv. 5–6)

Jesus' commentary on this widow's gift certainly was not, "This woman gave her last cent, and you should do likewise." The Lord does not want you to give up everything you have to live on. First Timothy 6:17 says He "richly supplies us with all things to enjoy."

The conclusion to it all was this: A false religion such as that led by the Pharisees, Sadducees, and scribes, which preys on the weak by holding out false hope in exchange for a monetary donation, is utterly corrupt and condemned.

Jesus foretells the destruction that will fall on these people because of their horrendous wickedness in verse 6, "As for these things which you are looking at, the days will come in which there will not be left one stone upon another which will not be torn down."

Jesus was angry, and this divine anger would

manifest itself against the leaders and the people, starting with the destruction of the Temple in AD 70 and lasting even until now. Because of the malfeasance of that false religion, the city of Jerusalem and nation of Israel has been devastated again and again, and will be until Christ returns.

CONTEMPORARY COMPARISONS

This kind of false religion did not stop with Judaism. In fact, the sixteenth-century Roman Catholic Church's abuse of the poor was so serious that it invalidated their entire religious system in Martin Luther's eyes.

At the time, Catholic leaders were building St. Peter's Basilica in Rome. They funded it by selling indulgences, promising the people that purchasing an indulgence would result in their sins being forgiven. Many who took the bait were the most impoverished and desperate people in society. But Rome was perfectly happy to fund their cathedrals with the exploitation of such hopeless people.

This is the corruption to which Luther reacted, spawning the Protestant Reformation.

You might notice that in cities all around the world, many Roman Catholic cathedrals are unfinished, and have been that way for hundreds of years. They are always in process. The reason for this is that the Roman Catholic Church can tax the people as long as construction continues. In fact, the history of the Roman Catholic Church consists of the accumulation of unimaginable wealth for the men at the top, funded from the pockets of the destitute who are trying to buy their way into heaven.

Perhaps more familiar to us are the prosperity preachers of the Charismatic movement, who promise all kinds of blessings to their listeners in exchange for their money. The largest demographic of donors to these "preachers" are single women who are desperate for the blessings promised—healing, wealth, or even a husband—as long as they send in their money.

That is not true religion and never has been. "Pure and undefiled religion in the sight of our God and Father is this: to visit orphans and widows in their distress" (Jas. 1:27). True religion does not abuse the poor. It graciously and generously ministers to their needs.

CONCLUSION

It is amazing that of all the little things that could have functioned as a trigger for the announcement of the Temple's destruction, our Lord put an account of an abused widow on the pages of Scripture. How terribly serious it is to abuse and exploit those who are distressed and helpless. It is even more serious to do it in the name of religion, or worse, the name of God.

The Lord cares for the downcast and the poor. He cares for those unable to provide for themselves. Jesus fed the crowds and healed the sick. He poured out love and grace on all who came to Him. He said that His yoke is easy and His burden, light. He was the antithesis of these religious leaders who walked all over the defenseless. To this day the Lord Jesus still calls the helpless sinner to salvation, not by monetary gifts, but by His grace alone through faith in Him.

FOCUSING ON
THE FACTS

1. What is the context of this passage? Why is it so important for getting the meaning right?

2. What are the lessons often taught *from* this passage? Why can we say those lessons are not taught *by* this text? What is the point of the passage?

3. What is the significance of what Jesus didn't say about the widow's gift? What is the significance of what He did say?

4. What does the account reveal about Jewish religion in Jesus' time?

5. Why is it significant that this event occurred immediately before the prophecy of the Temple's destruction?

6. What are some modern parallels to the greedy false religion of the Pharisees and Sadducees?

7. Based on Scripture, describe the attitude that the true church ought to have toward its widows.

PONDERING THE PRINCIPLES

1. Scripture identifies several marks of false teachers. One prominent mark in the New Testament is the love of money. In fact, Paul calls the love of money "a root of all sorts of evil" (1 Tim. 6:10). Paul warned Timothy severely about this danger: "Those who want to get rich fall into temptation and a snare and many foolish and harmful desires which plunge men into ruin and destruction" (v. 9). He goes so far as to say, "Some by longing for [money] have wandered away from the faith and pierced themselves with many griefs" (v. 10). Think about how the love of money can have devastating consequences, especially when it invades the church. Ask yourself whether you are free from the love of money. Paul commanded Timothy, "Flee from these things, you man of God, and pursue righteousness, godliness, faith, love, perseverance and gentleness" (v. 11).

2. Second Timothy 2:15 says, "Be diligent to present yourself approved to God as a workman who does not need to be ashamed, accurately handling the word of truth." Sometimes the context of a passage is *especially* important for understanding its meaning correctly. The isolation of the story in Luke 21:1–6 from the surrounding context of judgment has meant that it is frequently misunderstood as a lesson on giving rather than a rebuke of false religion. However, when the context is considered, the message becomes

clear. It is a reminder to make sure we interpret Bible passages in their context. Think of some practical ways you can be yet more diligent to accurately handle God's Word in your daily life, and seek to implement them.

THE CHILDLIKENESS OF BELIEVERS: CONFRONTING SIN

INTRODUCTION

A. Desiring the Lord's Blessing

I was very young when I first came to Grace Community Church. Many of our buildings—the worship center, the education building, the gym, the children's building—didn't exist yet. But it was a vibrant and energetic church, committed to Christ and excited for what the Lord had in store. A church calls a pastor with the assumption that he will be a blessing to them; it is a new beginning that brings with it the hope of growth and flourishing. And because the church had a passion to reach out and see people come to Christ, we all assumed the church would grow in this new phase.

1. A crucial text

> However, from the very beginning, I was not thinking about how to grow the church. It was never about how many people we could get into the building, or filling the few empty seats that there were in the chapel. I was never interested in making the church attractive. In fact, there was one prevailing text of Scripture that had settled in my mind: Matthew 18.

> It was probably two or three years before I came to Grace Church that I began to grapple with Matthew 18:15–20. Even a cursory reading of that text shows why it was such an important portion of Scripture to me as a young minister: "If your brother sins, go and show him his fault in private; if he listens to you, you have won your brother. But if he does not listen to you, take one or two more with you, so that by the mouth of two or three witnesses every fact may be confirmed. If he refuses to listen to them, tell it to the church; and if he refuses to listen even to the church, let him be to you as a Gentile and a tax collector. Truly I say to you, whatever you bind on earth shall have been bound in heaven; and whatever you loose on earth shall have been loosed in heaven. Again I say to you, that if two of you agree on earth about anything that they may ask, it shall be done for them by My Father

who is in heaven. For where two or three have gathered together in My name, I am there in their midst."

2. A disregarded practice

I found this passage difficult because I had never experienced, or even heard of a church that did what it said—people confronting each other about their sin, taking two or three witnesses with them, or telling the whole church about an impenitent member. The only part of it I ever heard quoted was verse 20, "Where two or three have gathered together in My name, I am there in their midst." And that was used as a popular axiom to remind people that even when only a few of them showed up for prayer meeting, God was with them.

The passage consumed my thinking. I read extensively on it and found commentators and theologians who explained the text, but I couldn't find anyone who actually applied it. In my naivete I asked some pastors if they had ever implemented this text or known anyone who did. The answer was a universal *no*.

3. A chief concern

But this passage contains Christ's first instructions to the church—His preeminent concern for the church is that it be dealing with sin within its own members. If it is the Lord's top priority, how can we read and understand Matthew 18:15–20, yet not implement it?

4. A fear of decline

I was told by much older and wiser men that if I tried to follow Jesus' prescription in this text, I would empty Grace Church. That folks wouldn't stand for it. "Do you think people in your church can walk up to others and confront their sin without driving them away? Do you think little groups of people can pursue a sinning believer without frightening everybody into leaving? You certainly don't think you can announce someone's sin to the whole congregation and have people come back the next week, do you?" They believed that if you want to add people to the church, you cannot put this into practice.

B. Demonstrating the Lord's Priority

1. A fearful event

But I was reminded of the famous account in Acts 5:1–11 of Ananias and his wife Sapphira. They were members of the Jerusalem church, and Ananias "sold a piece of property, and kept back some of the price for himself, with his wife's full knowledge" (vv. 1–2). Ananias didn't have to sell the property, but he freely chose to do so. He also had every right to keep whatever he wanted from that sale. There was no mandate from God to sell property and give all the proceeds to the church.

Verses 2–4 continue, "Bringing a portion of it, he laid it at the apostles' feet. But Peter said, 'Ananias, why has Satan filled your heart to lie to the Holy Spirit and to keep back some of the price of the land? While it remained unsold, did it not remain your own? And after it was sold, was it not under your control? Why is it that you have conceived this deed in your heart? You have not lied to men but to God.'"

What was the lie? That he was giving the entire proceeds of the sale to the church. He claimed to be giving everything for the work of the gospel. Peter told him that he didn't have to sell his property, nor did he have to give all of the money, nor did he have to lie about it. He had lied, not to men, but to God. "And as he heard these words, Ananias fell down and breathed his last" (v. 5).

Ananias dropped dead in front of the whole church, and *it was God who killed him.* Naturally, "Great fear came over all who heard of it" (v. 5). This seems like a great way to keep people out of the church—"Don't go there; people die!" Verse 6 says, "The young men got up and covered him up, and after carrying him out, they buried him."

The account continues with Sapphira: "Now

there elapsed an interval of about three hours, and his wife came in, not knowing what had happened. And Peter responded to her, 'Tell me whether you sold the land for such and such a price?' And she said, 'Yes, that was the price'" (vv. 7–8). This, of course, perpetuated the same lie her husband had told. So Peter confronted her, "'Why is it that you have agreed together to put the Spirit of the Lord to the test? Behold, the feet of those who have buried your husband are at the door, and they will carry you out as well.' And immediately she fell at his feet and breathed her last, and the young men came in and found her dead, and they carried her out and buried her beside her husband. And great fear came over the whole church, and over all who heard of these things" (vv. 9–11).

2. A divine method

What was the Lord trying to do? Did He want to prevent the church from growing? Wouldn't it have been better if the first instruction to the church in Matthew 18 created a warm and fuzzy environment for those who joined? At the very start of the church, the Lord dramatically and publicly executed two members for lying. That's not exactly putting out the welcome mat.

But a very important verse follows in Acts 5:13: "But none of the rest dared to associate with them; however, the people held them in high esteem." One of the church's objectives is to make our commitment to holiness so crystal clear that, on their own, people do not want to join. It should be so obvious that a church is devoted to righteousness that those who have no interest in virtue will not join.

The contemporary church's approach is the exact opposite. It minimizes its commitment to purity in order to present itself as all-accepting and welcoming, embracing anyone who walks through its doors. You may ask, "Otherwise, how can the church grow?" But verse 14 says of the Jerusalem church, "All the more believers in the Lord, multitudes of men and women, were constantly added to their number." Many evangelicals would love that to be their theme verse. Yet how did that growth happen in the Jerusalem church? The Lord openly killed two members for their sin in front of the church. That demonstrated a visible and resolute commitment to holiness. The church must be so faithfully obeying the Word of God that no natural man would want to join. Then, the church will grow legitimately because the Lord will be the one adding to His church.

Acts 2:47 says, "The Lord was adding to their number day by day those who were being saved." That is what the church is: a group of saved people. It is not a place that accommodates the unsaved. The unsaved should want to avoid it. It is not designed to make them feel comfortable.

C. Doing the Lord's Work

1. Taking Christ's headship seriously

A lot was at stake when I first came to Grace Church. I brought my precious wife and our children, and we wanted to be loved and wanted the work to flourish. We wanted to honor God. We didn't want to fail. We wanted more people to come and hear God's Word and be saved. We wanted to advance the gospel. But even then, I understood that it is the Lord who builds His church.

WHOSE CHURCH IS IT ANYWAY?

I remember when the church was growing rapidly in the early years, a reporter visited and asked me, "Do you have a great desire to build this church?" I responded, "Actually, I have no desire to build the church because Jesus said He would do that, and I don't want to compete with Him." Grace Community Church is not my church—it's His. I just want to know how He builds His church and get involved with that as His instrument. And it was very clear to me at that time that believers are called to maintain holiness in the church by dealing with sin—that that was a monumental issue.

The first time I met with the Grace Church elders, they asked me about doing a wedding for the daughter of a very prominent family that served in many capacities in the church. She was marrying an older, divorced man who was not a believer. So I told them I couldn't do it because it is wrong to marry a believer to an unbeliever. Someone replied, "That's going to offend them," and I said, "I feel badly about that, but there's someone I am more concerned about offending: the Lord of the church. I can't offend Him."

One of the men responded with, "OK, I understand that's your conviction. You don't have to do the wedding, but we can still have it here at Grace. That will make them feel better." Recall, this was our first meeting. But I said, "Is this your church? Whose church is this?" He answered, "It's the Lord's church." So I said, "Maybe we ought to do what the Lord wants done in His church." I couldn't do the wedding or have it on the church's campus because it is sinful to join a believer to an unbeliever.

That was a watershed moment. I said, "If this is Christ's church, and if it's going to honor Him, and if He's going to build it His way, then we have to obey His Word."

2. Taking sin seriously

It wasn't long before we started discussing the matter of church discipline as laid out in Matthew 18. As we did, I was warned that if I implemented that process, I would destroy Grace Church. And then, no other church would want me; I would become a ministerial pariah.

But I couldn't understand how you could preach against sin and not follow such an obvious pattern laid out in Scripture. How could you convince people that you are serious about sin if the only thing you ever did about it was preach? You can teach people God's view of sin from Scripture, illustrating and speaking passionately about it. But if you didn't carry out what the Bible prescribes for dealing with sin, why would anyone believe that you take sin seriously?

3. Taking the Bible seriously

But it goes deeper than that—if there were anything in Scripture that we were unwilling to abide by, then that is a severe breach in our integrity. We'd be selective in our submission to Scripture, and faithfulness leaves no room for that.

I am thankful for the influence of my grandfather, father, and mentors in seminary, but mostly for the influence of the Holy Spirit in my heart, which instilled in me an undying commitment to Scripture. The Bible isn't just true; it also must be obeyed as the only possible path for life. That's the only way to live as a joyful, productive Christian, and to be a church that the Lord Himself builds and is honored by.

I had been part of and seen many churches that preached against sin, but I had never seen one where they actually did something about it. And that just undermines everything you preach. If people see you as good at talking about sin but indifferent to dealing with it, you lack all integrity.

4. Taking our responsibility seriously

So even from the outset of my time at Grace Community Church, we were thinking through passages like Matthew 18:15–20 and Acts 5:1–11. We were thinking about 1 Corinthians 5:6, where Paul commanded the church to put out the immoral man because "a little leaven leavens the whole lump." We considered 2 Thessalonians 3:6, 11–15, where the church is told to eject disruptive believers, and 1 Timothy 1:20, where even leaders may be put out of the church. It seemed to me there was no way around this responsibility—we had to understand and obey Matthew 18.

LESSON

I. THE CHILDLIKENESS OF THE BELIEVER (MATT. 18:15)

A. Entering Like a Child

When Jesus spoke the words recorded in Matthew 18, He was in Capernaum, perhaps in Peter's home (cf. 17:24–25). And He had a little child on his lap as an illustration of the childlikeness of the believer (cf. Mark 9:36). He began this wonderful presentation by saying that we all enter the kingdom like children—if you do not become like a child, then you cannot enter the kingdom. We come in humble and dependent, without any accomplishment or achievement.

B. Disciplined Like a Child

Once we are in the kingdom, we remain as children. We need to be cared for and protected as children, as the first 14 verses teach. Now, in verse 15, He turns to say that we also need to be disciplined like children.

All of us desire a home free from undisciplined children. The prevalence of undisciplined homes today makes it obvious that children need to be disciplined—when they do what is wrong, they need to be confronted, corrected, and restored.

II. THE WORKERS OF DISCIPLINE

A. The Work of the Word

The Word of God itself disciplines us. It is "profitable for teaching, for reproof, for correction, for training in righteousness" (2 Tim. 3:16). Jesus said it is the Word that cuts, cleanses, and purges (Rev. 2:16; John 15:1–7; 17:17). It is the Word that washes (Eph. 5:26). It is the work of God's Word to purify the church by confronting sin, dealing with it, and showing the path of obedience and restoration.

B. The Work of the Spirit

Discipline is also the work of the Holy Spirit. The Spirit is none other than the Spirit of holiness who desires His church to be holy (cf. 1 Cor. 6:18–20). Thus, He does His sanctifying work in us.

C. The Work of the Church

Discipline is the work of the Word and of the Spirit of God. And it is to be our work, too. Paul wrote that he desired to present the church "as a pure virgin" (2 Cor. 11:2). Thus, it shouldn't surprise us that our Lord's first instruction to the church revealed His concern for the holiness, righteousness, purity, and obedience of His people.

My greatest grief over the state of the church today is its unholiness and its accommodation to the unsaved. Because of this sinful state that many churches are in, the application of Matthew 18 would initially seem destructive to those churches, but it would be to their ultimate benefit. Even so, it is unlikely to be widely practiced because Christian leaders aren't committed to obeying everything in God's Word. Yet this is the Lord's will for His church.

NO HIGHER COURT

Before we dig into the text, we should note that there is no higher court than the church. Here, "the church" refers to any duly constituted body of redeemed people. Jesus' words in Matthew 18 technically predate the beginning of the church on the day of Pentecost (Acts 2), but the body of believers was still an *ekklēsia*—a called-out assembly of God's redeemed people. So the instruction here was for those people assembled together in Capernaum, and it anticipated the official birth of the church in the near future. These instructions then became a mandate for the church's life.

Throughout history, all kinds of authorities have developed: popes, bishops, cardinals, synods, and so on. The New Testament knows nothing of those authorities. All it knows is a local church, which is an assembly of believers who have been called out of the world by God's efficacious, saving call.

In that sense, the local church is a body of believers who

are responsible to pursue their own holiness, and to care for one another in that pursuit. Christ's instructions for church discipline give the authority to that local assembly—there is no higher governing body. There may be times when a collection of ministers from outside a church has to move in and help, because that church has so defiled itself with sin and drifted into error that it is beyond its own capacities. But in God's design, the local church is the highest court.

III. THE PATTERN OF DISCIPLINE (MATT. 18:15–20)

The Lord lays out the plan for dealing with sin in the church as follows:

A. Reproving a Brother (v. 15*a*)

"If your brother sins, go and show him his fault in private . . ."

1. For what sins?

   This is not a difficult statement to understand. And when Jesus says "brother," He is not just speaking to the men—the term is representative of believing women too. People often ask what sins or what degree of sin this refers to, but Jesus doesn't specify because *any* sin is a defilement.

2. In what way?

Jesus also tells us to reprove in private. We're not to talk about it with other people, even though that is our natural tendency. Too often, we like to say, "Wow! Did you hear about what she did?" But that is not a biblical way of dealing with sin. In fact, that is in itself sin.

B. Winning a Brother (v. 15*b*)

". . . if he listens to you, you have won your brother."

Any sin is a defilement because it not only defiles the sinner and their personal relationships, but also the whole church, since we are one body.

But if the confronted believer "listens," which means he understands his sin, regrets it, and wants to turn from it, then "you have won your brother," Jesus says.

1. Recovery

Do you know that you can lose people inside the church? That's what the word "won" implies—you can't win them back if they weren't lost. The word "won" or "gained" (Gk., *kerdainō*) is actually a commercial word taken from the marketplace, and it gives us the purpose of this confrontation: to win the brother. Some people think that the point of church discipline is to throw people out of the church. It is not. The point is *to keep the people in the church pure.*

The verb "won" is sometimes used to refer to accumulating wealth in Scripture (cf. Matt. 16:26; Mark 8:36; Luke 9:25; Jas. 4:13). In this context it has the idea of the sinning brother being a loss to the fellowship, but becoming profitable once he is restored. He is like wealth regained or recovered.

Obviously, Jesus is not referring to sins of which believers repent and move on. He is talking about sins that we do not abandon—sins of which we do not repent. When someone follows this pattern of unrepentant sin, we have lost our brother or sister through that sin. So we go to recover him because he has value.

THE INESTIMABLE VALUE OF A BELIEVER

Every believer has value because the Spirit of God dwells in him and has gifted him for a ministry in the church. He is an instrument by which God can do His work in the church and in the world. This one sinning person is so valuable that we must endeavor to get him back. If he won't come back, then we take two or three others with us to try and get him back. If he still won't return, we must tell the whole church to pursue him because he has that much value. To restore him is to recover spiritual wealth.

G. Campbell Morgan once wrote, "It is the great tragedy of a man lost which colours all this instruction; and the purpose that is to be in our heart when we deal with a sinning brother, is that of gaining him. This word 'gain' suggests, not merely the effect on the one lost, but the value it creates for those who seek him. When presently we have done with the shadows and the mists of the little while, we will understand in the light of the undying ages that if we have gained one man we shall be richer than if we piled up all the wealth of the world. . . . What a blessed thing to gain a man, to possess him for oneself, for the fellowship of friends, for the enterprises of the Church, for the program of high heaven" (*The Gospel According to Matthew*, [New York: Fleming H. Revell Company, 1929], 232).

If you, as part of the church, are not willing to confront someone's sin, then you don't see them as valuable. But Christ does, because He paid the infinite price for them.

---

2. Responsibility

> The Lord gave us the responsibility to go after wandering children, like He holds parents responsible to pursue their own wandering children. My children are grown now, but discipline was a regular routine when we were raising them, and it was driven entirely by love. The fear was that they might be lost to us and to

the kingdom of God. So we disciplined them to make them feel the pain of their own sinfulness. Whenever they drifted into sin, we disciplined them for the purpose of restoration because they are priceless. You feel that way about your children, and our Lord is saying that you should feel the same way about the children of God.

3. Restoration

a. A spirit of compassion

Paul wrote in Galatians 6:1, "Brethren, even if anyone is caught in any trespass"—again, a very general instruction that relates to any sin. He continued, "You who are spiritual, restore such a one in a spirit of gentleness; each one looking to yourself, so that you too will not be tempted." We all understand what it is to be tempted and to sin. Thus, understanding human frailty, the power of temptation, and the residing flesh, we are to go after those in sin, desiring to restore them because of their value.

b. A spirit of helpfulness

The word "restore" (Gk., *katartizō*) means "to repair." It could be used of resetting fractures, or mending bones, or putting dislocated limbs back in place. This shows, again, that the point of dealing with sin is not to put people out. It's to restore them because of their value.

c. A spirit of gentleness

This restoration is to be done "in a spirit of gentleness." It is never to be harsh, but bathed in compassion, tenderness, sympathy, patience, and mercy because you understand what it is to be fallen—that's our universal experience.

4. Retrieval

Our model for this kind of discipline is God, as shown in the verses leading up to our passage in Matthew 18. Jesus said, "What do you think? If any man has a hundred sheep, and one of them has gone astray, does he not leave the ninety-nine on the mountains and go and search for the one that is straying? If it turns out that he finds it, truly I say to you, he rejoices over it more than over the ninety-nine which have not gone astray. So it is not the will of your Father who is in heaven that one of these little ones perish" (vv. 12–14).

When we pursue restoration, we're following God's own pattern. He goes after His sinning children to bring them back, even using us, His church, as the means to do that. Discipline is crucial because it is God's work.

C. Taking Witnesses (v. 16)

"But if he does not listen to you, take one or two more with you, so that by the mouth of two or three witnesses every fact may be confirmed."

This verse takes us back to the book of Deuteronomy where God established that accusations must be proven and attested by two or three witnesses (Deut. 19:15). Two or three witnesses were required to verify every fact.

So if the person doesn't respond to the first private confrontation, you take a couple of friends with you and confront him again, making sure that all the data is correct and calling him to repentance. This is done collectively, with the hope that he will listen and you will gain your brother.

D. Telling the Church (v. 17*a*)

"If he refuses to listen to them, tell it to the church . . ."

1. A joint effort

If the sinning church member doesn't heed the second confrontation either, we are commanded to tell the whole church. We are to tell the church that this person is living in a pattern of sin and that we have reproved him privately and then with a group, but he still won't repent. At this point we are not to shun the person; the whole church is to join in the effort to win them.

2. A noble end

Why would we go to this extreme? Because it is required and because it is noble. If you can be indifferent to someone's sin, then you don't care about that person. I have never been indifferent to the sins of the people I love. I want to do everything I can to restore them.

3. A loving call

In the church, we're called to love one another without restraint or boundary. So when someone is in sin, we tell the whole church. That isn't surprising, since the church is the collection of redeemed people. You are to tell the church about this person and his sin—not in lurid details, but to call them to go after that person. That's how valuable he is.

E. Putting Them Out (v. 17*b*)

". . . and if he refuses to listen even to the church, let him be to you as a Gentile and a tax collector."

1. Expelled members

In Jewish society, Gentiles were outcasts, and tax collectors were the most despised and despicable people. Tax collectors had sold their souls to Rome to gain a tax franchise by which they could extort money from their own people for a pagan, idolatrous nation. They were traitors. Jesus was saying that if a church member will not repent, we are to treat him like a total outcast and unbeliever.

2. Sinful contagion

   Why don't we accept such people into the fellowship? Because sin will leaven the church. There's so much more detail in this text, but suffice it to say that the church has to protect its holiness, and in an effort to protect its holiness, it calls the professing Christian back from sin. If that sinner doesn't respond to an individual, then two or three others join the effort. If he still does not repent, then you tell the church, and they collectively call him to restoration. If he continues to refuse, then put him out.

   First Corinthians 5:6 says, "A little leaven leavens the whole lump." You can't allow sinful influence to settle comfortably in the church. While I want Grace Community Church to be known as the loving congregation that it is, I also hope and pray that sinning people are never comfortable here.

3. Continual restoration

   I can tell you, personally, that if I were a professing Christian who wanted to live in sin, I wouldn't come to Grace Community Church. There have been people at Grace Church who profess faith in Christ, sin, are confronted and dealt with according to this pattern, and leave. We announce them when we have the Lord's Table on a Sunday morning. But most internal church discipline never reaches that point. It happens on an ongoing, one-on-one basis, with the result of restoration happening all the time, among families and friends.

This may be a hard thing to do, but it is not a hard instruction to understand. Remember that even the apostle Paul confronted none other than Peter. In fact, Paul confronted Peter to his face. Galatians 2:11 says, "But when Cephas came to Antioch, I opposed him to his face, because he stood condemned."

Can you imagine taking on Peter? Paul was a strong guy, but I'm certain he wasn't stronger than Peter. And I don't imagine it was easy to convince Peter of his own sin.

1. Consider the cost

   When you consider confronting someone about their sin, you might think, "This could end the relationship." That is possible. Regrettably, I have had that experience many times. I have confronted well-known pastors about serious errors in what I hope was a gracious manner, and it ended the relationship permanently. Perhaps you will pay that price.

2. Consider Christ's honor

   Was it worth it for Paul to confront Peter? Wouldn't it have been better if Paul just tried to cooperate with him? No. Paul did what was right for the sake of the honor of the Lord and of the church.

3. Consider the reward

Second Peter 3:14–15 tells us what happened to their relationship. Peter wrote, "Therefore, beloved, since you look for these things, be diligent to be found by Him in peace, spotless and blameless, and regard the patience of our Lord as salvation; just as also our beloved brother Paul . . . wrote to you." Paul was Peter's beloved brother because he had confronted Peter with the aim of restoring him.

F. Binding and Loosing (v. 18)

If this seems difficult, Matthew 18:18 offers further encouragement: "Truly I say to you, whatever you bind on earth shall have been bound in heaven; and whatever you loose on earth shall have been loosed in heaven."

This statement appears a number of times in the New Testament (Matt. 16:19; John 20:23) and has a simple idea. It might have been an axiomatic statement used by the rabbis. It simply means that when you bind something on earth it has *already* been bound in heaven, and when you loose something on earth it has *already* been loosed in heaven.

The rabbis said binding and loosing related to sin. If someone repented, then his sin was loosed, but if he would not repent, then he was bound in his sin. So when the church confronts a sinner but the sinner will not repent, and the church says that he is bound in his sin, heaven has already made that same judgment. On the other hand, when the church confronts a sinner and the sinner repents, and the church says he is loosed from his sin, they're only saying what heaven has already said.

The bottom line is this: When we confront sin, call people to repentance, hold them responsible for their impenitence, and rejoice with them in their restoration, we are simply doing on earth what has been done in heaven. We can truly pray, "Your will be done, on earth as it is in heaven" (Matt. 6:10). Heaven has already rendered the verdict that someone is either bound in sin or loosed from sin. We are just reflecting heaven's verdict when we do the same.

G. Agreeing with the Father (v. 19)

"Again I say to you, that if two of you agree on earth about anything that they may ask, it shall be done for them by My Father who is in heaven."

Jesus was saying that when two or three believers affirm someone's repentance, and heaven is in agreement, we can ask the Lord to cleanse and restore him, and God will. If the person will not repent, and heaven is in agreement, we can ask the Lord to chasten him, and God will. In other words, we're doing heaven's work.

H. Concurring with Christ (v. 20)

"For where two or three have gathered together in My name, I am there in their midst."

This does not refer to a prayer meeting. The Lord attends to the prayers of every single believer. Jesus said, "Lo, I am with you always" (Matt. 28:20). Matthew 18:20 concerns a discipline situation. The process is in motion with two or three people gathering together for that purpose. When that is the case, "I am there in their midst."

The church is never more in tune with Christ Himself than when it's dealing with sin, so we shouldn't be reluctant about doing this.

CONCLUSION

Church discipline didn't empty our church. The buildings were filled beyond their capacity, and we kept growing. Multitudes have come to believe in Christ and are continually being added to the church by the Lord. Grace Church is a place of love and restoration. It's a place of holiness and fear. That is exactly the way God designed it to be.

A. A Different Model

I love that people can't figure out how Grace Church grew. There is no human explanation, but the reason is clear: We are what we are because the Lord builds the church.

I remember many years ago, Fuller Seminary used to bring classes here from their church growth department, to examine our church. But one day, the head of the department called to say they wouldn't be coming anymore. Then he gave the reason: "Your church defies all analysis—it doesn't grow according to the principles of church growth." I was very glad that we couldn't be analyzed on a human level.

B. A Worldly Alternative

I'm sure when thousands of pastors come to this campus for Shepherds Conference each year, some in that mix of people would like me to tell them five things that guarantee a big church. And I could do that because that's easy: Soften up the message and pass out money. Or take the pulpit down and have a wrestling match up at the front. It's easy to draw a crowd.

I always wanted this church to be something that can only be divinely explained. That's why we just do what the Word of God tells us, and we let the Lord grow His church. It has been a joy and a delight to do so. I'm thankful for a congregation that pursues holiness and demonstrates the love of Christ to me, to my family, and to one another.

FOCUSING ON THE FACTS

1. Is it OK to want a church to grow? What are the pitfalls of seeking numerical growth in a church? What is the difference between God-given, supernatural growth and natural, worldly growth?

2. How is the issue of Christ's headship over the church related to implementing church discipline?

3. Why is the truth that Christ builds His church so fundamental for guiding a church's practice?

4. Why are so many churches reluctant to follow the pattern laid out in Matthew 18?

5. What does the account of Ananias and Sapphira demonstrate about the Lord's priorities for the church?

6. Explain the stages of church discipline that Jesus gives in Matthew 18:15–17. What is the purpose of church discipline? How does Jesus indicate this purpose in the text? How does church discipline protect the church?

7. What are some of the reasons you find it hard to confront sinning brothers and sisters? What truths can help you overcome the fear of confrontation?

8. How does Matthew 18:18–20 give encouragement to the church for dealing with sinning members?

PONDERING THE PRINCIPLES

1. Paul says in 1 Corinthians 1:18–31 that the Lord operates not according to the wisdom of this world but according to His own divine wisdom, which appears foolish to the world. The practice of church discipline is certainly something that the world, and worldly contingents of evangelicalism, see as foolish. But it is the wisdom of God. Take some time to think about how church discipline puts the wisdom of God on display, even before naysayers. Consider what it teaches us about God and His church. Consider also the spiritual benefits it brings to the church. In light of those realities, what practical steps might you personally need to take, as a believer responsible to call others to holiness?

2. Sometimes we are fearful to reprove other believers about their sin, feeling intimidated by how we think they might respond. It seems as if the loving thing to do is to ignore their sin. But that isn't loving as much as it is selfish and hard hearted. We have to remind ourselves of what James says: "My brethren, if any among you strays from the truth and one turns him back, let him know that he who turns a sinner from the error of his way will save his soul from death and will cover a multitude of sins" (Jas. 5:19–20). Love will drive us to rescue our brothers and sisters. Consider what these passages teach about reproof: Proverbs 9:8; 19:25; 27:5–6; Luke 17:3; Galatians 6:1; 1 Thessalonians 5:14; Titus 1:13; Jude 22–23; Revelation 3:19. Reflect

on how the principles in these passages shape the way you deal with sin in others.

STOP CRITICIZING

INTRODUCTION

"Do not judge so that you will not be judged. For in the way you judge, you will be judged; and by your standard of measure, it will be measured to you. Why do you look at the speck that is in your brother's eye, but do not notice the log that is in your own eye? Or how can you say to your brother, 'Let me take the speck out of your eye,' and behold, the log is in your own eye? You hypocrite, first take the log out of your own eye, and then you will see clearly to take the speck out of your brother's eye. Do not give what is holy to dogs, and do not throw your pearls before swine, or they will trample them under their feet, and turn and tear you to pieces" (Matt. 7:1–6).

This is a fascinating portion of Scripture, frequently referred to and often quoted, but not always understood in its totality as the Lord intended.

A. The Believer's Perspective

Up to this point of the Sermon on the Mount, our Lord has touched on all areas of the believer's life, summarizing different truths related to living in the kingdom. He began with the right perspective on self in the Beatitudes. He then gave the right perspective on the world in His statements about salt and light, and on the Word of God by teaching about God's law and the requirement of both internal and external devotion. He discussed our religious activity in giving, praying, and fasting, and our attitude toward money and material goods.

B. The Believer's Relationships

Now, in this passage, Jesus deals with our relationships. He has talked about how we relate to ourselves, God, His Word, the world, religious activity, the contemporary morality, and God's unchanging requirements. Now He speaks to our human relationships.

As in all the other elements of the Sermon on the Mount, the perspective here is given in contrast to the view of the scribes and the Pharisees, who were the prominent religious influences of the time. They were proud, but the Beatitudes taught humility. They were a part of the worldly system; Christ said that we are to be salt and light to such systems. They had denied the Word of God and established their own rules of religion; Christ reestablished the authority of His Word alone. They believed only in an external morality; Christ taught an internal morality. They performed their religious activities of giving, praying and fasting in a hypocritical, superficial way; the Lord said those must be done from the heart. They were preoccupied with money and possessions; the Lord said to be preoccupied not with earthly goods, but with God's kingdom.

Furthermore, the way they related to others was sinful, so the Lord had to set the record straight on that too. In contrasting them with Himself, He unmasked the inadequacy of human religion and reaffirmed the fact that true religion comes only from God.

Human relationships are the last topic Jesus addressed in His sermon before summarizing and concluding His message. The section dealing with such relationships extends from verses 1–12, but our focus is the first six verses.

C. The Jewish Leaders' System

1. Self-appointed judges

The Pharisees were so proud, self-righteous, and convinced of their superiority, that they naturally became hypercritical and condemning of everyone else.

That is always the case for a man or woman who

invents a system of morality. They inevitably become the judge sitting on the throne of that system, determining whether everyone else qualifies or not. The Pharisees had done this to the extent that they were oppressively judgmental of other people. They condemned and criticized. They were censorious. They were unmerciful, unforgiving, unkind, and lacking grace in their constant, carping criticism of everyone who didn't meet their own standard.

2. Superficial judges

Jesus told those religious leaders, "Do not judge according to appearance, but judge with righteous judgment" (John 7:24), precisely because it was their habit to judge very superficially.

3. Self-deceived judges

Luke 16:14–15 says, "Now the Pharisees, who were lovers of money, were listening to all these things and were scoffing at Him. And He said to them, 'You are those who justify yourselves in the sight of men, but God knows your hearts; for that which is highly esteemed among men is detestable in the sight of God.'" Jesus was saying to them, "You think you have the answers. You think your system is a pure religion; you think you are the judges. But you are wrong." Their judgments were the reverse of God's judgments.

4. Self-righteous judges

Luke 18 gives a classic illustration of their problem. "[Jesus] also told this parable to some people who trusted in themselves that they were righteous, and viewed others with contempt" (v. 9). That's a reference to the Pharisees, who put all of their confidence in self-righteousness. Because they had set themselves up as the standard of righteousness and because of their pride and egotism, they despised and looked down on everyone else. So the Lord confronts them with this parable.

"Two men went up into the temple to pray, one a Pharisee and the other a tax collector" (v. 10). From the Pharisees' viewpoint, a tax collector was the most wretched, vile person in society because he had aligned himself with the interests of Rome to collect taxes on their behalf, and he would rip off the Jewish population in doing so. He was a traitor of the first order.

The ESV translates verse 11, "The Pharisee, standing by himself, prayed thus: 'God, I thank you that I am not like other men, extortioners, unjust, adulterers, or even like this tax collector.'" The Pharisee wasn't interested in associating with anyone else because no one attained to his level. He found a place where he could stand alone, separated from others, to demonstrate his unparalleled self-righteousness. And he said, "'I thank You that I am not like . . . this tax collector. I fast twice a week; I pay tithes of all that I get.' But the tax collector, standing some distance away, was even unwilling to lift up his eyes to heaven, but was beating his breast, saying, 'God, be merciful to me, the sinner!' I tell you, this man went to his house justified rather than the other" (vv. 11–14).

The Pharisees made judgments, but their judgments were wrong. The main feature of their dealings with others was their condemning attitude. And that fact betrayed their claim to be citizens of God's kingdom—you can't have that kind of attitude as a true believer.

The Lord recognized this pervasive problem among the Pharisees and spoke to it in Matthew 7.

LESSON

In Matthew 7:1–12, Jesus delivers the Sermon on the Mount's conclusive teaching on human interactions. Who could sum all of that up in just twelve verses? There are books on behavioral psychology ad infinitum, ad nauseam, trying to determine how human relations should be coordinated. But Jesus, in a simple manner, says more in twelve verses than all of those volumes put together.

Verses 1–6 explain how we are *not* to deal with one another—that's the negative instruction. Then, verses 7–12 cover how we *are* to deal with one another—that's the positive instruction. The sum of the negative and positive instructions is enough to govern ll our human relations.

If you want to know how to act in your family, job, neighborhood, recreation, or busness, this section summarizes it all.

This lesson covers the negative part of Jesus' instruction—that is, what not to do in your relationships with others. The overall principle appears in verse 1: "Do not judge." You might object, "You can't reduce all of human relations to that one principle." But you can.

I. WHETHER TO JUDGE

Many people have misunderstood this command. For example, Russian novelist Leo Tolstoy wrote, "[Christ's] words 'judge not' are directed precisely against the institutions of any [human] courts of law" (*What I Believe* [1885; repr., Cosimo, Inc., 2007], 27). That is a gross misinterpretation, but others have made aberrations of equal magnitude. For instance, many say that we should never criticize. They think we should never judge anything or anyone, lest we also be judged.

That is the spirit of our age—we live in a time that

hates theology and dogma. People resist doctrine and avoid convictions. They speak of love, compromise, ecumenism, unity; they want whatever will get everyone together. That makes somebody who even discusses doctrine widely unpopular.

"NO DOCTRINE, PLEASE!"

Once, we received a call from a church looking for a young man who might want to candidate for their pulpit. They said, "We want someone who will teach holiness, not doctrine." Our age resists conviction. Our time is opposed to strong men who will speak up, confront society, and disturb the status quo. Men who know what they believe, why they believe it, and are not intimidated to say it are branded as controversial troublemakers.

That same week, I was asked to review a book whose thesis was that we have to eliminate doctrine from Christianity and go all out for love and fellowship instead. It claimed that doctrine, and those committed to it, was the culprit dividing the body of Christ.

Contrast that with the church historically—it praised men for being men of conviction. Being a man of principle, of standards, of dogma was honorable. If there hadn't been such men, then there wouldn't have been a Reformation. But today, such men are considered difficult, uncooperative, self-styled, and unloving. The man this age praises is the compromiser.

Thus, many people impose the contemporary, anti-doctrine and anti-conviction mentality onto the command "Judge not."

The Lord is obviously not condemning law courts; the Bible instituted them. The principle of "an eye for an eye, and a tooth for a tooth," to which He just referred, was based on a God-ordained law court (Matt. 5:38; cf. Ex. 21:24; Lev. 24:20; Deut. 19:21). Also, Romans 13:1–7 and 1 Peter 2:13–17 affirm the right of a nation to rule its people according to a system of law.

Neither does the Bible condemn all kinds of judgment or discrimination. In fact, Scripture commands believers to discern truth from falsehood.

II. HOW TO JUDGE

A. Its Necessity

The whole Sermon on the Mount is predicated on a clear understanding of the distinction between true and false religion—between hypocrisy and reality. We cannot be undiscriminating; we cannot be blind, flabby sentimentalists.

1. Discerning the enemy

For example, verse 6 reads, "Do not give what

is holy to dogs, and do not throw your pearls before swine." To apply this passage, you will have to find out who the hogs are and who the dogs are, so that you can act accordingly. You have to discriminate.

Look at verse 15: "Beware of the false prophets, who come to you in sheep's clothing." If you settle for a superficial perception, all you'll see is sheep's clothing and never recognize the wolf underneath. You have to discern. If you do not judge, then you won't be able to avoid the false prophets because you won't know who they are.

So within this passage itself we are told to test, evaluate, and discriminate between true and false.

2. Disciplining the brethren

In this same gospel, the church is told to confront a sinning brother boldly and forthrightly about his sin, and to make it a public issue to the church if he does not repent (Matt. 18:15–20). That does not allow us to be flexible in our obedience to Scripture—we are called to discern.

3. Damning the heretic

Paul likewise showed that there is a legitimate kind of judgment when he wrote, "If any man is preaching to you a gospel contrary to what you received, he is to be accursed!" (Gal. 1:9). John said that anyone who does not preach the Christ of the Bible "is the deceiver and the antichrist," and he added, "Do not receive him into your house, and do not give him a greeting; for the one who gives him a greeting participates in his evil deeds" (2 John 7, 10–11).

4. Excluding the corrupt

In 1 Corinthians 5, we are told to remove those who are sinning from our midst because they are like leaven that leavens the whole lump of dough. Hymenaeus and Alexander were put out of the church because of their corrupting influence upon it (1 Tim. 1:20).

Throughout the whole Bible we are commanded to discern, to try the spirits, to have our senses trained so that we know the difference between good and evil (Heb. 5:14; 1 John 4:1–6).

B. Its Nature

Hence, we know that the command "Judge not" doesn't mean we shouldn't discriminate between truth and error. Ephesians 4:14 says it is a child who doesn't know the difference between true and false, and thus becomes preyed upon "by every wind of doctrine, by the trickery of men, by craftiness in deceitful scheming." We must discern. We must judge. That's not what the Lord is decrying.

Instead, Jesus is disavowing the critical, self-righteous egotism of the Pharisees. They weren't criticizing people because of sin. They were criticizing people for their personalities and weaknesses—perhaps even the way they looked or dressed. They criticized people for not living in the same way as them. They judged people's motives, which they did not and could not know.

1. Loving judgment

The Lord is not saying, "Accept everyone the way they are, and never judge them." In fact, Leviticus 19:17 says, "You shall not hate your brother in your heart; you may surely reprove your neighbor, and so not bear sin because of him" (LSB). To allow another to sin is to hate him, not love him. So if you see sin, it is love that calls for repentance.

People say, "I don't want to say anything. I just want to love everyone." But if you tolerate someone's sin, you are hating him. Love confronts, while hate ignores a sin and lets a person continue in that path.

2. Righteous judgment

Jesus Himself evaluated, condemned, judged, and criticized repeatedly. He unmasked the hypocrisy of the Pharisees with a scathing diatribe in Matthew 23. So His words in Matthew 7 were not referring to judgment of every kind. He was talking about the ugly, condemning spirit of the Pharisees—and all who are like them.

3. Distinguishing judgment

We must judge. Romans 16:17 tells us, "Keep your eye on those who cause dissensions and hindrances contrary to the teaching which you learned, and turn away from them." We must make doctrinal distinctions, mark the people who offend that doctrine, and avoid those people. We have a right to "judge with righteous judgment" (John 7:24), but not to issue carping criticisms, like the Pharisees.

4. Contrasting judgment

The word "judge" in Matthew 7:1 translates the Greek word *krinō*, and it could potentially be translated as many as twenty different ways. So its breadth of meaning requires that context be the deciding factor in how we interpret it.

The context of the sermon in Matthew 7 is the contrast with the Pharisees. Again, when we consider the biblical context more broadly, we know Jesus is not forbidding all judgment, because in many other places He tells of its necessity. But righteous judgment is the opposite of Pharisaical judgment.

III. HOW NOT TO JUDGE

We are not to judge people's motives. We are not to

condemn them because they don't look or act or talk like we think they should. We are not to judge them because they don't come up to our own self-righteous standard. That is forbidden.

Romans 14:13 succinctly says, "Let us not judge one another anymore." *Stop criticizing.*

The Bible is very clear about the kind of judging that is sinful.

A. Vengeful Judgment

First, we're not to take legal judgments into our own hands. Jesus mentioned the legal prescription of "an eye for an eye, and a tooth for a tooth" just two chapters earlier, in Matthew 5, not for it to be administered in personal relationships but in a court of law. There's no place in the Bible for taking personal vengeance (cf. Lev. 19:18; Rom. 12:19).

B. Hasty Judgment

The Bible also forbids hasty judgments. Proverbs 18:13, "He who gives an answer before he hears, it is folly and shame to him." Scripture commands us not to pass judgments with less than full knowledge of the facts.

C. Unwarranted Judgment

We're not to make unwarranted or undeserved judgments, such as those which Paul prohibited in Colossians 2:16 regarding the observance of feasts, new moons, and Sabbaths. We cannot set up our own human standard and then look down on people when they do not live up to our non-biblical code.

D. Unjust Judgment

Nor are we to make unjust judgments, as the judges in the Northern Kingdom of Israel did. They accepted bribes and judged with partiality (cf. Deut. 10:17; 16:19; Micah 3:9–10; Jas. 2:1–9).

E. Unmerciful Judgment

Nor are we to judge unmercifully, with persistent, unrelenting criticism. God doesn't judge that way; He is rich in mercy (cf. Ps. 130:3–4; Eph. 2:4).

F. Slanderous Judgment

So the kind of judgment the Lord is forbidding here is a vengeful, hasty, unwarranted, unjust, and unmerciful condemnation spawned by self-righteous pride. But even worse is if, having made such a judgment in our hearts, we then proceed to tell others about it and become a tale-bearer and a gossip (cf. Lev. 19:16; Prov. 18:8; 20:19; 2 Cor. 12:20).

IV. WHY NOT TO JUDGE (MATT. 7:1–4)

In this passage, the Lord gives us three reasons we are not to make such judgments.

A. It Manifests a Wrong View of God (v. 1)

"Do not judge so that you will not be judged."

Jesus reminds us by this verse that we are not the final court. He essentially asked them, "Have you forgotten that *you are not God*?" Because that is the bottom line with this sin. To judge other people, their motives and so forth, is to play God. It's to usurp His divine position.

1. Usurping the Son

John 5:22–30 tells us that judgment belongs to God, and He's committed it to the Son—that's as far as it reaches. We are not, at this particular time, to sit in judgment. The Bible tells us that there will come a time in the millennium when we will join the Lord in His reign and judgment, but we do not presently have that right.

2. Usurping God

Think of it this way: Every time you sit in judgment on someone or criticize their motives, you're playing God. Every time you take up a personal vendetta and seek vengeance, every time you try to get even on your own, you are playing God. Every time you pass a sentence on someone arbitrarily, you're playing God.

That is not the case if you are confronting an obvious sin and follow the biblical principles of church discipline. It is only true when you set yourself up as the authority that determines the standard for others to meet. Whenever you do so, you have taken God's seat.

3. Usurping the Master

Romans 14:4—Paul wrote, "Who are you to judge the servant of another?" In other words, the believer is God's servant, not yours. And it is "to his own master he stands or falls."

4. Usurping the Omniscient

1 Corinthians 4:3–5—"To me it is a very small thing that I may be examined by you, or by any human court; in fact, I do not even examine myself. For I am conscious of nothing against myself, yet I am not by this acquitted; but the one who examines me is the Lord. Therefore do not go on passing judgment before the time, but wait until the Lord comes who will both bring to light the things hidden in the darkness and disclose the motives of men's hearts; and then each man's praise will come to him from God." We often sit in judgment on other people's ministries, lives, or attitudes, but Jesus was saying that if we eliminate that kind of judgment, we will dramatically alter our human relationships.

5. Usurping the Lawgiver

James 4:11–12—James spoke directly to this issue: "Do not speak against one another, brethren. He who speaks against a brother or judges his brother, speaks against the law and judges the law; but if you judge the law, you are not a doer of the law but a judge of it. There is only one Lawgiver and Judge, the One who is able to save and to destroy; but who are you who judge your neighbor?" We must not usurp God's position by setting ourselves above the law as its judges rather than living as its subjects.

Every time you criticize someone because they don't do something the way you think it should be done, or because you think you know their motive, you pass judgment as if you were God. In the words of one writer:

> Judge not; the workings of his brain
> And of his heart thou canst not see;
> What looks to thy dim eyes a stain,
> In God's pure light may only be
> A scar, brought from some well-won field,
> Where thou wouldst only faint and yield.
> (Adelaide Anne Procter, "Judge Not," *The Complete Poetical Works of Adelaide Anne Procter* [Boston: Houghton, Mifflin, 1901], 7–8).

Don't play God.

B. It Manifests a Wrong View of Others (v. 2)

"For in the way you judge, you will be judged; and by your standard of measure, it will be measured to you."

Most people think they can judge because they are not under the standard that applies to everyone else. The Pharisees thought they were exempt from the law and beyond the purview of judgment, that they were above the law and everyone else was below it. But Jesus told them that they, like all of us, would get what they gave.

1. Judged by God

   Some think this verse is about human relationships: that if you judge someone, that person will judge you in the same way, with the same measure. That is true to some extent, as Luke 6:38 indicates—there is typically reciprocity in the way we treat others.

   But that's not the point of this verse. How men treat us is not what motivates us. As we noted, Paul said in 1 Corinthians 4:3 that it is a small thing when men judge us. A man or woman who walks with God is less concerned about what men think versus what God thinks. The great restriction on our life is how God views us.

   Certainly, we are not indifferent to what men think. As Proverbs 27:6 says, "Faithful are the wounds of a friend"; or Psalm 141:5, "Let the righteous smite me in kindness and reprove me." Yet more than anything else, we seek God's approval.

2. Judged by knowledge

Jesus was referring to God's judgment. He was saying, "The judgment with which you judge, God will judge you with. And the measure with which you measure, God will use to measure to you." God is going to evaluate you on the basis of your knowledge. If you claim to know enough to judge everyone else, then you prove you know enough to be judged yourself.

a. Luke 12:48—Jesus said, "From everyone who has been given much, much will be required."

b. Hebrews 10:29—"How much severer punishment do you think he will deserve who has trampled under foot the Son of God, and has regarded as unclean the blood of the covenant by which he was sanctified, and has insulted the Spirit of grace?" The more you know, the more you're responsible for.

c. James 3:1—James made a pertinent point when he wrote, "Let not many of you become teachers, my brethren, knowing that as such we will incur a stricter judgment." The one who teaches shows himself to be knowledgeable, and he will be judged according to that knowledge. The more you know, the severer the judgment.

Jesus said to the crowd, "You might think that by knowing so much, you sit in an impervious seat of judgment, but in actuality, you make yourself responsible to live up to that standard."

3. Judged by one standard

Those who judged in this sinful manner had a wrong view of others. They thought that they were exempt and everyone else would be condemned. But there is no double standard with Jesus. People will be judged according to how they judge everyone else.

In Romans 2:1 Paul spoke similarly: "You have no excuse, everyone of you who passes judgment, for in that which you judge another, you condemn yourself; for you who judge practice the same things." By judging others, a person proves that he knows better than to do the things for which he condemns them. Thus, when he also does those things, he will likewise be condemned, being judged according to his knowledge.

There is no double standard with God. We should not criticize, because in criticizing we assume we are exempt though others are not. Thus, we demonstrate a wrong view of others—that they are under us, rather than equal to us. But God will judge us by the same standard with which we judge them.

4. Judged by our own judgment

If you're characterized by negativity, gossip, talebearing, criticism, and judgment, then you are under the illusion that you are beyond judgment. But whenever you condemn someone else, you prove that you must likewise be condemned for the same things in your own life. Criticism is a boomerang which, when thrown at others, returns to you. Unloving criticism will backfire on you by the hand of God.

Haman, from the book of Esther, illustrates this perfectly. He built a gallows in order to hang Mordecai but ended up being hanged on his own gallows instead. Similarly, there was a king named Adoni-bezek in Judges 1 who had captured seventy kings, and cut off their thumbs and big toes. But then he was captured, and his own thumbs and big toes were cut off. He summed up his lot by saying, "As I have done, so God has repaid me" (v. 7).

To judge is to play God, thinking that you are on your own moral plane, exalted above everyone else. Your own self-righteousness and ego will cloud your judgment so that you can't judge righteously.

THE GRAVITY OF JUDGMENT

The story is told of Sisamnes, a judge in Persia who was

once bribed to render the wrong verdict. When the Persian king, Cambyses, heard that the judge had succumbed to the bribe, he ordered that Sisamnes be executed, flayed, and that the judgment seat be covered with his skin. He then appointed Sisamnes's son, Otanes, to replace him as judge. From that point on, Otanes and every judge in that court in Persia rendered judgment while sitting on that chair. That is a graphic reminder of the importance of judging fairly.

If we are not careful, our own egos will make us prejudiced, and our ignorance will make us impotent in judgment. We have no business thinking that we operate by a different standard than everyone else.

C. It Manifests a Wrong View of Self (vv. 3–4)

"Why do you look at the speck that is in your brother's eye, but do not notice the log that is in your own eye? Or how can you say to your brother, 'Let me take the speck out of your eye,' and behold, the log is in your own eye?"

When you critically judge other people, you demonstrate an erroneous view of yourself. You're doing so well that you have nothing to work on yourself, so you can spend your time evaluating everyone else?

Some of us would do well to take the time we spend

criticizing other people, and devote it to private prayer and confession of our own sin. Because until we get our own lives straight, we are of very little use in assisting others.

1. A comical illustration

That is essentially what the Lord said in verses 3–4: "Why do you look at the speck that is in your brother's eye . . . ?" The "speck" refers to something like a splinter, twig, or wood chip. The idea is that it's not enormous, but it's not so tiny that it isn't painful. It is something substantial that, if caught in your eye, would cause significant discomfort.

On the other hand, Jesus said, "[You] do not notice the log that is in your own eye." A "log" here is like a large beam that supports a ceiling.

Jesus pictures this almost cartoonishly. We all know it's very irritating to have even a tiny object in our eyes, but here is a man with a splinter in his eye—that would be miserable. Then along comes another man who wants to help remove the splinter, but he has an eight-foot two-by-four protruding from *his* eye. He can't even get close to the man with the splinter, let alone see well enough to locate the sliver properly.

So Jesus says in verse 4, "How can you say to your brother, 'Let me take the speck out of your eye,' and behold, the log is in your own eye?" That would be ridiculous.

We are unfit judges, not only because we can't play the part of God and because we tend to think ourselves under a different standard than everyone else, but also because we are utterly blind in our perception of the situation. Whenever we judge or criticize someone, we prove that we are blind—because if we could see, we'd first attend to the plank in our own eye instead of someone else's splinter.

2. A crippling condition

People have argued back and forth about what the splinter and the plank refer to, and some have said the splinter is a little sin. But it can't be, because having a wood chip in your eye is a terrible condition to be in; it must depict a fairly severe sin. Then they say that the plank is an especially vile sin. But that doesn't follow either. People with such wicked sins usually don't try to straighten out other people with less serious sins than themselves—they usually prefer to justify such people, and themselves.

The people who see everything wrong in the lives of others typically see nothing wrong in their own life—and the only sin that sees no wrong in its own life is self-righteousness. That is what the plank represents. As long as you are self-righteous or spiritually proud, and set yourself up as a judge, you can't help anyone with their sin.

It is interesting that the Lord's caricature depicts such self-righteousness as a far worse sin than any other. It is the vilest of all sins because it plays God. It denies the gospel because it denies the need for redemption.

So long as you have that plank of self-righteousness and never bother dealing with your own sin, then you are of no use to anyone else. You are blind with the subtle sin of self-righteous criticism.

3. A consuming preoccupation

If you are focused on the principle of righteousness, then you will deal with your own sin, not the other person's. If you are actually concerned about righteousness, judgment, and truth, then that concern will appear in your own life first. If you have the perception to know truth and righteousness, and a hunger for them, then you will see sin where it is most obvious—your own heart.

The Beatitudes are critical to understanding this section. It is only when you humbly thirst for righteousness out of a recognition of your sinfulness that you can heed Jesus' words here. Someone who is truly holy is preoccupied with his own sinfulness—he's not trying to pull splinters out of other people's eyes while he has a plank in his own eye.

So Jesus says to each one who would judge this way, "You hypocrite" (v. 5). He was calling such people phonies and pretenders—those who would be eye doctors but had never treated their own eyes.

V. WHY TO JUDGE (MATT. 7:5–6)

Two dangers immediately arise when we respond to all this by saying, "I'm not going to judge; I'm just going to take care of my own life and leave everyone else alone." First, we become unwilling to confront a sinning brother. We might be tempted to think, "Who am I to tell others how they should live—'Judge not, lest ye be judged!'" Or, second, we might be tempted not to discern or discriminate at all. In this case we think, "I don't want to recognize anything as false or erroneous, so I'll just take it all in."

Yet both of those would devastate the church with sin and false teaching. We will let the enemy in because of our unwillingness to discriminate between truth and error.

So the two dangers are that we might fail to deal with a brother in sin and that we might fail to deal with a heretic. The Lord closes with a masterful injunction to address both of those dangers.

A. The Necessity of Confrontation (v. 5)

1. Confession

". . . first take the log out of your own eye . . ."

The Lord does not conclude His instruction simply with, "You have a log in your eye." He continues, "*Take the log out* of your eye." He is calling for you to eradicate self-righteousness and pride.

It's a matter of confessing sin. First, you have to recognize that the sin is there, as verse 3 says, "Do [you] not notice the log that is in your own eye?" The word "notice" means to perceive in a meditative way. It is used in Luke 12:27 in Jesus' command, "*Consider* the lilies" (emphasis added) and in James 1:23, "He is like a man who *looks* . . . in a mirror" (emphasis added). It is a long look of understanding. Jesus is saying, "Take a good look at yourself, and notice your spiritual problem. Consider that you have an ungodly, self-righteous attitude that makes you judgmental and critical of others."

Then, having considered and recognized your sin, cast it out by confessing it to the Lord. As 1 Corinthians 11:31 says, "If we judged ourselves rightly, we would not be judged." God will not have to chasten us for self-righteousness if we deal with it. We must bring our lives fully before Him and ask Him to cleanse and purify us of our pride.

2. Correction

". . . and then you will see clearly to take the speck out of your brother's eye."

Once we have confessed our own sin, we move on to the second half of this verse, which calls us to remove the splinter from our brother's eye. To let him continue in sin would be to hate him (Lev. 19:17).

David wrote of this in Psalm 51: "Create in me a clean heart, O God . . . . Then I will teach transgressors Your ways, and sinners will be converted to You" (vv. 10, 13). There is no way to effectively teach a transgressor until you have a clean heart yourself.

When the Lord told us not to judge, He wasn't telling us not to help a sinning brother. He was telling us to get our own act together first because then our help will be the right kind of help—humble and meek. As Paul wrote in Galatians 6:1, "If anyone is caught in any trespass . . . restore such a one in a spirit of gentleness; each one looking to yourself, so that you too will not be tempted." We are not to come to a sinning brother from above, but underneath, in humility.

Jesus told Peter in Luke 22, "Satan has demanded permission to sift you like wheat; but

I have prayed for you, that your faith may not fail; and you, when once you have turned again, strengthen your brothers" (vv. 31–32). Peter couldn't strengthen the brethren until his own life was right.

As Galatians 6:1 says, we need to be in a sound spiritual state before we can help others—and the key to that is selfless, humble love. We are not to be a judge, playing God. We're not to be superior, thinking there's a double standard. We're not to be a hypocrite, condemning everyone else while blind to the sin in our own life. But we are to be a brother—having dealt with our sin, we help others out of brotherly love.

B. The Necessity of Discernment (v. 6)

"Do not give what is holy to dogs, and do not throw your pearls before swine, or they will trample them under their feet, and turn and tear you to pieces."

Returning to the second danger, in our day many people want to say, "'Judge not, lest ye be judged'— we don't want to discriminate or hold anyone to doctrinal standards. We just want everyone to get together and love each other." But Matthew 7:6 explodes that mindset.

1. Dirty dogs

Dogs in those days were not the pampered little, nice-smelling, dolled up lapdogs that we see today. Apart from the trained sheep dogs that worked with the flocks, they were mostly ugly mongrels that scavenged around the city in wild packs and ate garbage.

a. An unclean animal

The Jews believed dogs were unclean. The Psalms describe them as threatening, howling, snarling, greedy, and shameless (cf. Pss. 22:16–20; 59:6–7, 14–15). They were contemptible. They were savage pariahs that lived in the garbage heaps. Obviously, holy things were not to be thrown to the dogs.

b. A consecrated offering

When someone went to the Temple to offer a sacrifice to the Lord, he would take part of it home, part would go to the priest for his meal, and part would go on the altar. The part that went on the altar was for God, and it was consumed on the altar as an offering to the Lord (Lev. 3; 7:11–15; Num. 18:8, 11).

No priest would take the part on the altar, even for himself. He might throw the leftover bones from his own portion to the dogs, or the person who brought the sacrifice might do the same with the bones left over from his part; but they would never take that which was offered to God on the altar and throw it to the dogs. That would be a horrible desecration by a filthy, vile animal.

c. A discriminating ministry

Everyone knew that you don't throw the holy part of a sacrifice to a bunch of wild dogs. Similarly, the Lord was telling them to be discriminating in ministry because there are some people who will hear your critiques and respond to you. But there are others on whom you shouldn't waste precious truth because they will tear it to pieces, utterly ignorant of its significance.

Dogs were so detestable in those days; they were known even to eat people. That was Jezebel's fate when she was thrown from a window—the dogs rushed over and devoured her. They were such vile animals that it was considered a curse to be eaten by dogs (1 Kings 21:19–24; 2 Kings 9:33–37).

2. Savage swine

Jesus also told His audience not to throw pearls before swine because they would trample the pearls under their feet and become angry enough to tear those people up. The pigs of those days were not as domesticated as the pigs you might meet on a farm today. If you upset a drove of pigs, you could be in a lot of trouble.

a. A priceless treasure

No one would pretend to feed pigs by throwing pearls to them instead of food—a man would have had to liquidate his entire fortune to get just one pearl from the Persian Sea or Indian Ocean. They were priceless.

b. A senseless beast

No one would throw a pearl to a hog because a hog can't appreciate a pearl. It will think the pearl is a big piece of barley, and when it realizes it isn't, it'll turn on you. Don't waste precious things on those who don't appreciate them. That requires you to discern who those people are and to discriminate accordingly.

c. A discriminating ministry

This is a tremendous truth: We have to be discriminating in our ministry. That means we are selective in what we say and whom we say it to. Even Paul followed this principle when he said to the Corinthians, "I, brethren, could not speak to you as to spiritual men, but as to men of flesh, as to infants in Christ" (1 Cor. 3:1).

Likewise, Jesus only revealed certain things to His disciples, and hid other things from them. And of the world, He said, "I praise You, Father, Lord of heaven and earth, that You have hidden these things from the wise and intelligent and have revealed them to infants"

(Matt. 11:25). When He rose from the dead, Jesus never once appeared to an unbeliever.

Hogs were the chosen refuge of the demons in Matthew 8. They were contemptible and filthy in Jewish eyes. In fact, Jesus depicted the lowest point of the prodigal son's horrid life as his living with pigs and eating their slop—to show he had reached the pits, in Jewish culture. God designated pigs unclean (Deut. 14:8).

3. Depraved defectors

But who is Jesus calling hogs and dogs? Second Peter 2 says, "False prophets also arose among the people, just as there will also be false teachers among you . . . . Many will follow their sensuality" (vv. 1–2).

That speaks of all who follow the ways of false teachers and thus involve themselves in false systems of religion. They are covetous, lustful, evil, vile, just like those drowned in the Flood, or like those destroyed in Sodom and Gomorrah for their homosexuality (vv. 5–6). They "indulge the flesh in its corrupt desires," are "self-willed," and "revile angelic majesties" (v. 10). They are stains and blemishes (v. 13).

Peter calls them "accursed children . . . having followed the way of Balaam" (vv. 14–15), "springs without water" (v. 17), who "escaped the defilements of the world by the [head] knowledge of the Lord and Savior Jesus Christ" (v. 20) yet "turn away from the holy commandment" (v. 21). Then the apostle closes with this statement: "It has happened to them according to the true proverb, 'A dog returns to its own vomit,' and, 'A sow, after washing, returns to wallowing in the mire'" (v. 22).

You could take a street dog into your home and improve his diet, but he will still immediately go back to his vomit. You could do the same for a hog—take it in, clean it up—but if you leave the door open, it will go back out to its slop.

The dogs and the pigs are those who, having known the truth, willfully turn from it to embrace the way of false teachers. And we should not allow them to trample under their evil feet the purity of the gospel message. It is not always easy to distinguish for ourselves who's reached the level of being a hog or a dog, so we need to rely on the Lord to reveal it.

4. Shrewd servants

   a. Matthew 10:14—When Jesus sent out the disciples, He instructed them, "Whoever does not receive you, nor heed your words, as you go out of that house or that city, shake the dust off your feet."

   Jesus was patient with Peter, Thomas, and His

other disciples, but He didn't say anything to Herod Antipas. He knew Herod had a hard heart, so He didn't waste pearls on him.

b. Acts 18:6–7—Paul, after one instance of preaching to the Jews, "when they resisted and blasphemed, he shook out his garments and said to them, 'Your blood be on your own heads! I am clean. From now on I will go to the Gentiles.' Then he left there." He just abandoned them like that? Well, some of them were saved in the end, but they were saved by coming to the gospel, not by the gospel coming to them. Paul did turn his back and walk out.

c. 2 John 9–11—The aged apostle John wrote to the church not to welcome or support any teacher of a false system—not meaning that we should not evangelize unbelievers, even cult members. His point was "not [to] give him a greeting" as if he were part of the fellowship of true believers, and "not [to] receive him into your house" or provide him any other kind of sustenance which might further his blasphemous ministry. Don't throw what is holy to dogs—don't let them trample the pearls.

So what are the "holy things" and "pearls"? Without a doubt they signify the Word of God. They are God's truth, including the gospel and all the contents of Scripture.

Sometimes I am invited to speak in a setting where the audience is made up of unbelievers. When I do, I am always very careful how I use the Bible because I know there are truths they will mock, despise, and reject. I don't want to give them the opportunity to mistreat the precious treasures of God's Word.

CONCLUSION

We must make judgments, but they must be righteous judgments. We must discriminate and deal with the sins of our brothers and sisters, but we must not have a judgmental and critical attitude. If we do, we set ourselves up as a self-righteous judge.

It all comes down to our attitude. The key question to consider is whether you are criticizing, evaluating, discerning, and discriminating *in order to know the truth and honor God*. Or are you doing it to exalt yourself and hurt someone else? That is the determinative factor.

The Lord has been so gracious as to forgive us—He is far more merciful with us than we are with others. May we also be tenderhearted, kind, and forgiving, standing for the truth and living with discernment, but not from a self-righteous, self-serving heart. And when we find those who err, may we restore them in love and meekness.

FOCUSING ON THE FACTS

1. How have you seen Matthew 7:1 misused? How could you respond to correct such misunderstandings of this passage?

2. How does Matthew 7:2–6 help interpret verse 1 correctly?

3. What does a hypercritical person reveal about their view of God, others, and themselves? How does their perspective on those three areas compare with biblical truth?

4. How does an awareness of God's way of judging shape how we judge others? Support your answer with specific passages of Scripture.

5. What does "the speck" represent (v. 3)? What about "the log"? Why is the log so serious?

6. What does it mean to "take the log out of your own eye" (v. 5)? Why does this position us well to help our brother or sister?

7. Whom did Jesus label as "dogs" and "pigs"? How do we know this? Who would fit that description in our day?

8. How does the principle of verse 6 control the way you teach sacred truths to others? Cross-reference other passages of Scripture to support your answer.

PONDERING THE PRINCIPLES

1. The command to "judge not" can be misapplied in many different directions. In a lot of cases, people use it as a license to avoid all discernment and confrontation. Others use it to justify themselves when challenged about their sin. Still others simply brush it aside, thinking it does not apply to them. Consider what pitfalls you are prone to regarding this command— you may be inclined to avoid all forms of judging, or you may lean toward a hypercritical and judgmental attitude. But it's likely that you fall into both errors, at different times. Spend time reflecting on how the Bible teaches us to be discerning *and* gracious Christians, and identify specific circumstances and relationships in your life where you can begin to apply those principles today.

2. We live in an age that is averse to reproof and correction. Even within the church, there is a constant pressure to speak positively about everyone. In fact, you might wonder what people would think today if they heard Jesus call certain people dogs and swine! Sometimes it feels like the biggest sin in today's church is criticism. But a reticence to biblically call out evil has left the church in a dangerous position— heresy and sin run rampant, while Christians sit on their hands for fear of being judgmental. Recall, Jesus' instructions were not to cease from all judgment; they were to refrain from hypocritical, self-righteous

judgment. So are you following the Bible's pattern for dealing with sin and error, or are you letting fear of man bully you into silence? Study again Scripture's passages which explain why, when, and how we must correct one another; look also at those which teach us why purity in the church is so paramount. Examine yourself carefully, to see how you may better align yourself with God's own priorities.

CONFIDENCE IN GOD'S WORD, AS IT IS WRITTEN

INTRODUCTION

Our focus together during this time is going to be on a passage that is in your Bible but shouldn't be.

A. The Overarching Goal

On Sunday, June 5, 2011, I completed an endeavor that began in February of 1969. From the time I arrived at Grace Community Church on that February 9, my desire was to teach through the New Testament, and I had prepared for that task. I'd taken a Greek minor in college and a New Testament emphasis in seminary. I wanted to preach verse by verse through the New Testament with a reasonable measure of depth—not taking every rabbit trail, but being fair to the content of each text.

The years had gone by since 1969, and on June 5, 2011, I finished preaching through the New Testament, averaging 5.5 verses per message in the gospels and 4 verses per message in the epistles. And at the end of that undertaking, I believed, as I did when I started, that I held in my hand the living Word of God. Not only that, but every message I preached was the Word of God, insofar as I had correctly interpreted Scripture.

B. The Governing Method

1. Defending Scripture

I could have begun the forty-three-year effort with a long defense of Scripture's authenticity, authority, inspiration, inerrancy, or sufficiency. And while through the years I talked about those truths as they arose in the text, I didn't begin with that long defense. That's because I believe that Scripture is its own defense. When it is examined and understood, the Bible will make its own case for authority and inerrancy. I am a presuppositionalist in that sense.

God doesn't try to prove that the Bible is true; He simply declares the truth. I have never tried to prove to the congregation of Grace Church that the Bible is God's Word. I don't need to because Scripture is its own peerless advocate. Its accuracy, truthfulness, and power are obvious as its content accumulates. Its weight ever increases to its students, while doubt diminishes and disappears.

For those who aren't exposed regularly to the truth and power of Scripture, some rational defenses may help. But for those who are regularly and systematically brought into the depths of holy Scripture, it builds its own case. Eventually, you have something like concrete reinforced with rebar that you can stand on—a foundation that does not move.

2. Explaining Scripture

I only had one objective in my exposition of the New Testament, and it wasn't homiletical—I don't think I ever spent more than fifteen minutes on an outline. It wasn't practical—I don't spend a lot of time thinking of practical applications for the message, since everyone's different. It wasn't cultural—I didn't try to figure out how I could make a passage say what the culture wanted it to say. I never thought about relevance. I never thought about how I might move people's emotions. I never thought about how I could motivate them.

All I thought about was how to explain what the text means.

The best way to describe my preaching for those years would be *explanatory*. My commentaries reflect that. You won't find any dead German heretics in my commentaries because I don't care what they think; I just care what God thinks.

3. Interpreting Scripture

The key question I had to answer was: *What does Scripture mean by what it says?* From there, the Holy Spirit moves with power where and in whom He wills, based upon a right understanding of Holy Scripture.

For some years I preached four sermons a Sunday, then, for many years, three sermons a Sunday (two in the morning, one at night, from two different books), but my struggle was always the same: What does the passage mean? And once you ascertain the meaning of the text and reinforce that truth with Scripture's teaching as a whole, then, out of the living and powerful truth of Scripture, comes divine, compelling, life-changing implications. The Holy Spirit will apply the message—I want people to feel the burden of the implications.

4. Enjoying Scripture

I confess that over those forty-three years I always found myself caught up in the joy of this exercise. While it took hard work and self-discipline, it was never a drudgery. Even in the midst of self-examination that threatened my sense of well-being, even when I discovered issues in my own heart that had to be addressed, the joy was always there. With that joy, love for God, and delight in His Word, came an ever-increasing passion.

5. Obeying Scripture

I wanted my people to know the joy and love that comes from understanding God's Word and its implications. I knew that their response to every truth would either result in blessing or judgment, and I wanted them to have blessing. So while my desire was to explain the meaning of Scripture, I couldn't keep passion out of it, and I still can't to this day because it is the fire of my heart. I desire for God's people to see the implications of Scripture, step into the realm of obedience, and experience God's blessing.

6. Preaching Scripture

So, from February 1969 until June 2011, that's what I did—I preached through the New Testament. I never planned the order in which I would preach the books. I didn't go from the first chapter of Matthew to the last chapter of Revelation. The order, from a human perspective, was random—and included sections from the Old Testament. I simply thought, "I would like to know this book," so I did it. Of course, the

Lord was behind the scenes, ordering it all by His providence, but I didn't have any particular plan.

C. The Unusual Conclusion

As I approached the end of Luke in my preaching, Mark was the only book left. And I thought, "These people have been in Luke for ten years; they're going to be upset when I tell them we're going to start over again in Mark!" But I miscalculated their response. When I announced that we would go through Mark, the whole church responded with joy—and that joy lasted all the way through the end of the book.

For many preachers, Mark is the starting point because it's like a newspaper version of the life of Christ. It's short, to the point, and has very few didactic sections. The story is told rapidly, with the frequent repetition of the word "immediately."

But at the end of forty-three years of exposition, I landed in the final verses of the book of Mark and had to tell my people that something was in their Bibles that shouldn't be.

1. The empty tomb

Mark ended his powerful history of our Lord Jesus as the other gospel writers did: with the Resurrection. Matthew, Luke, and John, of course, relate some of the appearances of Christ after the Resurrection, but they all essentially end with that monumental event. Mark does the same, and gives the testimony that Jesus is alive with the news of the empty tomb in 16:1–5. Then in verses 5–7, the angels testify that He's alive. And then, in verse 8, the women go on their way to give their eyewitness testimony to the apostles.

Thus, Mark ends his account with the testimony of the empty tomb, the testimony of the angels, and the testimony of eyewitnesses. Verse 8 says, "They went out and fled from the tomb, for trembling and astonishment had gripped them; and they said nothing to anyone, for they were afraid."

2. The astonished witnesses

"They were afraid" translates the passive form of the verb *phobeō*, which, for example, Homer used to speak of fleeing or being put to flight. Perhaps we should translate the word that way so we're not thinking of them as scared. We are given the reason that they fled: to tell the disciples that Jesus was alive.

Mark ends abruptly, with trembling, astonishment, and awe. The women were overwhelmed and stunned into silence. So was Mark, and he dropped his quill.

3. The abrupt ending

   I've written a few books through the years, and as a writer, if I had submitted a conclusion like that, I would probably get a note back from the publisher: "This is too abrupt; you need to add more here."

   So more was added to Mark. You can probably see in your Bible the little brackets around verses 9–20, and then another bracketed section after verse 20—those indicate the additions.

4. The obvious questions

   There I was, after forty-three years of teaching the Word of God, and we all end up in a very confusing place. Is this section of Mark's gospel, which appears in our Bibles, not supposed to be here? And how many other sections are like that? It seemed like I faced the task of preaching my last sermon from a text that wasn't supposed to be there. And it posed the question, Is my Bible accurate? Is my copy trustworthy?

   This brought the question of confidence in Scripture directly to the surface. I assumed it for decades, and so did my people. We loved the Word of God and didn't question it for forty-three years—but did this text change anything?

5. The encouraging answers

   This all led me to do a postscript message on this

passage on a Sunday night, after preaching up to verse 8 that morning. And I found this section provided a rich opportunity for Bible students to be strengthened in their confidence in the Bible as the Word of God. Examining this section does the opposite of what we might expect—it gives the Bible reader an opportunity to understand their cherished English translation. And more than that, it gives an insight into the history of ancient texts on which modern texts are based.

I. THE PRESERVATION OF SCRIPTURE[1]

Beneath the surface of your cherished Bible is a long history of careful preservation. We don't have the first autographs, that is, the original documents written by the first and only authors of Scripture. But we have carefully preserved copies of those autographs from very close to the time they were written.

This passage of Scripture gives us the opportunity to take a look at the meticulous way in which God's Word has been preserved. In fact, the New Testament, the portion of Scripture most recently recorded, has been accurately maintained for two thousand years.

A. Determining the Original Text

The study of ancient copies (sometimes called textual criticism), is the first step in interpreting

---

1   All stats throughout this section have been updated per Clay Jones, "The Bibliographical Test Updated," Christian Research Institute, updated April 12, 2023, https://www.equip.org/articles/the-bibliographical-test-updated/.

God's holy revelation. It is not my area of expertise, but there are those who devote their lives to it, and they are our benefactors.

The first question to ask when considering various manuscripts is, What did God actually write? What did the original, Spirit-inspired writings consist of? Then I, as a pastor, come along sometime later and study the text that has been handed down and explain what it means.

B. Studying the Sources

All translations of Scripture are based on ancient sources, which have been discovered and studied by fastidious scholars through the centuries to determine the accuracy of those sources. Thousands of people involved in such activity have given abundant affirmation to the fact that the Holy Spirit not only inspired Scripture but also preserved it in all its purity.

Ancient scribes knew they were copying out the very words of God. Since the printing press was not built until 1440, copies before then were written by hand with great caution. Those craftsmen understood the gravity of their task.

C. Considering the Witnesses

Because of Scripture's preeminence, it has been copied and translated far more than any other work of literature. There are a total of around

25,000 textual witnesses (complete and fragmented Greek manuscripts plus ancient translations to other languages) to the New Testament. Such an abundance preserved by the Holy Spirit through faithful men makes it possible to reconstruct the original books with virtually complete accuracy.

There is no work of ancient literature that even approaches the New Testament in its quantity of manuscripts or in the uniform consistency of the text over the centuries.

1. Greek manuscripts

   There are more than 5,600 Greek manuscripts containing some or all of the New Testament—and they date back to the second century.

   a. Papyri

      For example, we have a fragment of John's gospel labeled Papyrus 52 that was written from around AD 100–150. Another set of manuscripts, the Bodmer Papyri, include Luke, John, Jude, and Peter's epistles and can all be dated to the second and third centuries. You might have heard of the Chester Beatty Papyri—these manuscripts contain large portions of all four gospels, many of the Pauline epistles, and a portion of Revelation from sometime in the third century.

      It is remarkable that any of the manuscripts

from that era survived, since it was period of intense persecution for Christians, which included the destruction of copies of Scripture.

b. Codices

When Christianity was granted freedom in the Roman Empire by Constantine I in AD 313, believers no longer faced the same persecution, which enabled the proliferation of biblical manuscripts.

One such early and important text is Codex Sinaiticus. This codex contains the entire New Testament (and most of the Old) and dates to the fourth century—maybe about AD 350. Another text, perhaps slightly older than Sinaiticus, is Codex Vaticanus—it contains most of the New Testament and most of the Old. And of special note: In both of those ancient manuscripts, Mark's gospel ends at 16:8.

2. Translations

a. Latin

There are more than 8,000 copies of Jerome's Vulgate from across the centuries. This was a Latin translation of the Bible that Jerome undertook from AD 382–405. "Vulgate" means "common" in Latin; Jerome's Vulgate became the common translation of the Bible in use.

b. Syriac

More than 350 manuscripts of Syriac translations exist today, some of which date to the fifth and sixth centuries and represent a text from as early as the AD 200s. Syriac is a dialect of Aramaic—probably similar to the language Jesus spoke. It's from the regions that Syria, Turkey, and Iraq occupy today.

All of these facts demonstrate that the original text of Scripture has been protected and preserved down to this day. And we would expect no less from the Holy Spirit, who inspired it in the first place.

D. Comparing with the Classics

No work of ancient literature has anywhere near as much manuscript evidence as the New Testament.

1. Second to the New Testament's (approximately) 5,600 Greek manuscripts is Homer's *Iliad*, of which there are currently around 1,800 manuscripts. The *Iliad* was probably written in the eighth century BC, but the earliest manuscript dates only to the fourth century BC—400 years after it was written. (The earliest complete manuscript dates only to the tenth century AD). But the oldest New Testament manuscripts reach back to the second century—only shortly after it was written.

2. About 250 manuscripts of Caesar's *Gallic Wars* exist today. The earliest of these manuscripts is from the ninth century AD—about 1,000 years after it was written in the first century BC.

3. Herodotus's *History of the Persian Wars* was written in the fifth century BC and a little over 100 of its manuscripts are known today. The earliest extant manuscript of this work is from the tenth century AD—about 1,300 years after the original.

4. The *History of the Peloponnesian War* by Thucydides currently has about 100 manuscripts. It was written in the fifth century BC, and while some fragments exist from the third century BC, it relies mostly on manuscripts from 1,300 years after it was written.

E. Marveling at the Accuracy

The Bible surpasses all of those ancient works with its number of accurate, consistent manuscripts. We can know with certainty that we hold in our hands an English translation of the original with no appreciable variation. No less a scholar than A. T. Robertson said that the vast array of New Testament manuscripts has enabled textual scholars to ascertain the original text with as much as 99.9% accuracy (Fenton J. A. Hort and Brooke F. Wescott, introduction and appendix to *The New Testament in the Original Greek*, vol. 2 [New York: Macmillan

& Co., 1896], 2, quoted in A. T. Robertson, *An Introduction to the Textual Criticism of the New Testament* [Nashville: Sunday School Board of the Sothern Baptist Convention, 1925], 22).

F. Identifying the Variants

Variations exist in ancient manuscripts because they were handwritten. Errors occurred here and there in inadvertent mistakes or omissions, or an attempted clarification every now and then. But they are minor and inconsequential—and they are known. In most modern translations you will see an alternate reading in the margin indicating where such a variant exists. Scholars examine the manuscripts to determine the original reading and inform us which reading is most likely correct—typically that appears in the text of your Bible, while the alternate (less likely) reading is in the margin. But the variants are not hidden, so that we know what they are and that they are not detrimental to the text.

II. THE ENDING OF MARK

I say all of the above because the end of Mark, as it appears in your Bibles, has a long textual variant that was not originally part of Mark's gospel. Usually, in our English translations, verses 9–20 appear in brackets, followed by an additional italicized portion in brackets. That is because it is widely recognized that these portions were not in the autograph.

A. The Motive for an Added Ending

So why is this section here? The rather obvious reason is that the actual ending seems too abrupt. The brief and stunning ending of Mark's carefully crafted history of the Lord Jesus Christ prompted such an addition. Mark's description is dramatic—there is trembling, astonishment, speechlessness, fear, and awe. The women are in a state of terrified bewilderment, gripped by the wondrous reality of the Resurrection. They know Jesus is alive; they were there—the tomb was empty, and the angels declared it. They are speechless, and so is Mark.

It is fitting that this gospel has such a dramatic and powerful ending—the women could not speak, and Mark could not write. Mark had said what needed to be said. The evidence was in, and the point of his gospel was proven: Jesus is who Mark said He was in Mark 1:1: "The beginning of the gospel of Jesus Christ, the Son of God." The case was closed.

B. The Hypotheses for the Sudden Ending

Many commentators have suggested reasons why Mark didn't write a longer ending.

1. Mark's deference to Luke

For instance, some suggest that Mark interacted with Luke since they were in Rome together at the same time. They think that since Luke's gospel had already been penned, and it gave an extensive post-Resurrection history, Mark decided not to do the same.

2. The execution of Peter

   Others suggest that Peter was Mark's source (which is most likely true, based on the testimony of the church father Papias), and that Peter was executed before Mark could write his conclusion. So Mark could not finish the gospel.

3. The availability of other gospels

   Another theory claims that Matthew, Luke, and Acts had all already been written with details of Jesus' post-Resurrection appearances. Thus, much like John, who omitted the pre-baptism history of Jesus, Mark omitted the post-Resurrection history.

4. Mark's focus in writing

   Some say that Mark didn't write about the end of Jesus' life in the same way he didn't write about the beginning; he skipped to the middle because that was his focus.

5. Mark's fast-paced approach

   Yet another option is that Mark liked to be brief and to use few words, so he thought this conclusion was enough and decided to stop.

6. An open ending

Some even say that Mark intended to leave the ending open—like a rhetorical device to encourage the reader to write their own ending.

7. A lost ending

Finally, there is the theory that Mark did write a longer ending, but it is lost. Commentators will go so far as to write several pages about a supposed lost ending. But think about that. If such an ending has never been found, then these writers don't know it exists; and even if it did exist, it's lost, so they can't know what's in it.

All of the above theories are speculation. We don't know Mark's motives or circumstances. We certainly don't know anything about a lost ending. All we have is Mark and his words. The women fled from the tomb trembling, astonished, and silent (v. 8). It may be a shocking ending, but it's not incomplete.

Yet apparently certain people in the early church thought it was. Somewhere along the line, they started writing additional endings which made their way into the text. Those endings are identified by the brackets that appear in your Bible.

C. The External Evidence for the Sudden Ending

1. A rejected shorter ending

   You can see a short italicized portion in your Bible, probably at the end of chapter 16—that has been rejected by the overwhelming majority as having no connection to Mark.

2. A spurious longer ending

   The end of verse 18 indicates that Onesiphorus also actively ministered to the church at Ephesus. We don't know what his specific role was; he could have been an elder or pastor also. Whatever role he had, the quality of his character and service was well known to Timothy.

   a. Incomplete source material

      Then there is the longer ending in brackets, from verses 9–20. That has been included in some translations, like the King James, that didn't have the benefit of earlier manuscripts which were discovered after it was translated. The limited collection of later manuscripts that those translations are based on is called the Textus Receptus.

      Verses 9–20 have been considered legitimate by some, but they are not in the oldest manuscripts. Thus, in modern translations, the section is put within brackets to indicate that it is not original.

b. Early witnesses

As we have learned, our translations of the Bible are based on ancient Greek manuscripts. The original documents (called the autographs) do not exist, but early copies of them do. And the bracketed passage at the end of Mark 16 does not appear in the earliest copies. It is not in Sinaiticus or Vaticanus. Eusebius and Jerome wrote in the fourth century AD that almost all Greek manuscripts ended with verse 8. But Justin Martyr and Tatian show knowledge of other endings in the second century AD, and Irenaeus quotes 16:19 from the spurious section.

So these endings were added very early in the history of the church, but they were not universally accepted. Many medieval manuscripts, which were the basis for some English translations, included them; but that was before the oldest manuscripts were discovered. Thus, they appear in English Bibles like the King James Version.

D. The Internal Evidence for the Sudden Ending

So there's a strong case based on external evidence for excluding this passage. But let's also consider the internal evidence, that is, the content of the text itself.

1. An awkward transition

   First, the transition in verse 9 is strange, awkward: "Now after He had risen early on the first day of the week, He first appeared to Mary Magdalene." "Now" seems to indicate continuity (or contrast) with the preceding verse, but what follows in verse 9 doesn't continue the story of verse 8. The women went out, fled from the tomb with trembling and astonishment, and were silent. Then verse 9 introduces "He," but whom does that refer to? "He" is a masculine pronoun, but there is no "He" antecedent in the prior section—only the women.

   And then there is the odd introduction, "Mary Magdalene, from whom He had cast out seven demons." But Mary has already appeared three times in this section of the account (Mark 15:40, 47; 16:1)—she needs no introduction by now.

2. A mismatched location

   In verse 7, the angels say that Jesus would appear to the disciples in Galilee, but the appearances described in verses 9–20 are in (or near) Jerusalem (cf. Luke 24:13–49).

3. A change in vocabulary and structure

   Furthermore, verses 9–20 have vocabulary not used anywhere else in Mark. There are at least eighteen terms used here that never appear elsewhere in this gospel. The structure of this section, too, differs from what is typical of Mark's writing in the rest of his gospel. For example, the title "Lord Jesus" appears in verse 19 but nowhere else in Mark.

4. An absent disciple

Peter is singled out by the angel in verse 7 to go to Galilee and meet with Jesus, and he is most likely Mark's source for the gospel, yet Peter is not mentioned in verses 9–20.

5. A foreign theme

Finally, the subject of miraculous signs with snakes and poison is nowhere in any gospel.

E. The Sources for the Longer Ending

We do not know where this ending came from. However, we can tell that verse 9 is a summary of Luke 8:1–3; verse 10 is borrowed from John 20:18; verse 12 comes from Luke 24:13–34; verses 13 and 14 from Luke 24:35–43; verse 15 from Matthew 28:19 and Acts 1:8; verse 16 from John 20:23. And verses 17–18 are a strange combination of some of the promises of miraculous power the Lord made to the disciples in Matthew 10, Mark 6, and Luke 10, with some of the phenomena that occurred in the book of Acts and 1 Corinthians.

So this ending was put together after the fact, as a

summary, to give the gospel of Mark a less abrupt conclusion.

F. The Explanation for the Sudden Ending

But why did Mark end his gospel where he did? Let's return to the beginning of the book.

1. A foreshadowed ending

    a. Mark 1:16–22—Jesus was walking by the sea and saw Simon, Andrew, James, and John, and called them to follow Him (vv. 16–20). Then "they went into Capernaum; and immediately on the Sabbath He entered the synagogue and began to teach. They were *amazed* at His teaching" (vv. 21–22, emphasis added).

    b. Mark 1:25–27—Jesus cast out a demon, and "they were all *amazed*" (v. 27, emphasis added).

    c. Mark 2:11–12—Jesus heals the paralytic and forgives his sins. He addressed the paralytic, "'I say to you, get up, pick up your pallet and go home.' And he got up and immediately picked up the pallet and went out in the sight of everyone, so that they were all *amazed* and were glorifying God, saying, 'We have never seen anything like this'" (emphasis added).

    d. Mark 4:37–41—Jesus was in a boat during a fierce gale, with waves breaking over the boat (v. 37). The boat was filling up with water, but

Jesus was so weary that He was in the stern, asleep. The disciples "woke Him and said to Him, 'Teacher, do You not care that we are perishing?' And He got up and rebuked the wind and said to the sea, 'Hush, be still.' And the wind died down and it became perfectly calm. And He said to them, 'Why are you afraid? Do you still have no faith?' They became *very much afraid* and said to one another, 'Who then is this, that even the wind and the sea obey Him?'" (vv. 38–41, emphasis added).

e. Mark 5:15—After Jesus healed a demoniac, the people "came to Jesus and observed the man who had been demon-possessed sitting down, clothed and in his right mind, the very man who had had the 'legion'; and they *became frightened*" (emphasis added).

f. Mark 5:27–33—Mark recounts the story of the woman who touched Jesus' garment and was healed (vv. 27–29). Verse 33 describes her response: "The woman *fearing* and *trembling*, aware of what had happened to her, came and fell down before Him and told Him the whole truth" (emphasis added).

g. Mark 5:41–42—Jesus raised a girl from the dead, saying to her, "'Talitha kum!' (which translated means, 'Little girl, I say to you, get up!'). Immediately the girl got up and began to walk, for she was twelve years old. And immediately they were *completely astounded*" (emphasis added).

h. Mark 6:51—"He got into the boat with [the disciples], and the wind stopped; and they were *utterly astonished*" (emphasis added).

i. Mark 9:6—When Jesus was transfigured, the three disciples "became *terrified*" (emphasis added).

j. Mark 9:15—The scribes were arguing with His disciples, and when the crowd "saw [Jesus], they were *amazed* and began running up to greet Him" (emphasis added).

k. Mark 9:31–32—Jesus taught the disciples, "'The Son of Man is to be delivered into the hands of men, and they will kill Him; and when He has been killed, He will rise three days later.' But they did not understand this statement, and they *were afraid* to ask Him" (emphasis added).

l. Mark 10:24—"The disciples were amazed at His words."

m. Mark 10:32—"They were on the road going up to Jerusalem, and Jesus was walking on ahead of them; and they *were amazed*, and those who followed were *fearful*" (emphasis added).

n. Mark 11:18—"The chief priests and the scribes heard this, and began seeking how to destroy Him; they *were afraid* of Him, for the whole crowd was astonished at His teaching" (emphasis added).

o. Mark 12:17—Jesus said, "'Render to Caesar the things that are Caesar's, and to God the things that are God's.' And they *were amazed* at Him" (emphasis added).

p. Mark 15:4–5—One of the most remarkable reactions to Jesus was from Pilate when he questioned Jesus. When Jesus gave no answer, "Pilate was amazed" (v. 5).

q. Mark 16:4–8—Finally, the women arrive at the tomb and "Looking up, they saw that the stone had been rolled away, although it was extremely large. Entering the tomb, they saw a young man sitting at the right, wearing a white robe; and they *were amazed*" (vv. 4–5, emphasis added).

And then in verse 8, Mark writes, "They went out and fled from the tomb, for *trembling* and *astonishment* had gripped them; and they said nothing to anyone, for they were *afraid*" (emphasis added).

2. A fitting ending

I can't think of a better ending for Mark's gospel: the amazing Jesus.

It ends as it began, with amazement over the Lord Jesus Christ. And when you stop where Mark stopped, you step back in awe of the amazing Jesus. Every lesson, every miracle, every stunning answer, every insight, every righteous word, every holy act, fills you with stunning amazement.

You should be speechless like the women—and like Mark—at the amazing Jesus.

CONCLUSION

That's how it was for us at Grace Community Church when we reached the end of Mark.

But it didn't take long for people to ask me what we were going to do next. We had been studying Jesus for forty-three years in the New Testament—historically in the gospels and Acts, theologically in the epistles, and eschatologically in Revelation. But what was next? Surprisingly, people asked me to go back to the gospel of John—they could not get enough of the amazing Jesus.

A. The Church's Need for Christ

If there's anything missing in the preaching of the church today, it is Jesus Christ. There are too many quirky, novel, homiletical talks about how to fix your life and elevate your comfort zone. The gaping hole in the modern church's preaching is the absence of Jesus Christ.

But the apostle Paul said, "I determined to know nothing among you except Jesus Christ, and Him crucified" (1 Cor. 2:2). If you preach the gospels, you preach the history of Christ. If you preach the epistles, you preach the theology concerning Christ. If you preach Revelation, you preach the eschatological presentation of Christ. But you will always preach Christ.

B. The Old Testament's Testimony to Christ

So after preaching the through New Testament, I told the people that there was somewhere we hadn't preached Christ from—the Old Testament. I decided to go back to the Old Testament and find Him prophetically.

My grandchildren play a game called Where's Waldo? You can't find Waldo if you don't know what he looks like, but if you know what he looks like, you can find him. And after forty-three years, we knew what Jesus looks like, so we could find Him in the Old Testament.

If we only had the Old Testament, we would still have the veil over our face (2 Cor. 3:13–14). That veil is removed in Christ, so now we can see Him everywhere He appears. We can look back and see Him immediately in the Old Testament, as early as

Genesis 1, because He's the Creator God.

C. The Bible's Theme Is Christ

On the road to Emmaus, the Lord Jesus said that the Old Testament revealed Him (Luke 24:25), "Then beginning with Moses and with all the prophets, He explained to them the things concerning Himself in all the Scriptures" (v. 27). The apostles and prophets who preached the gospel in the first generation of the church preached from the Old Testament—it was the only Bible they had. Even the writers of the New Testament based their writings on the Old Testament. The revelation of the amazing glory of Christ begins there and continues through every page of Scripture.

FOCUSING ON THE FACTS

1. What is the best way to defend the truth of Scripture?

2. Why does preaching revolve around interpreting the passage correctly and explaining its meaning? What are the dangers of style-driven or application-driven preaching?

3. What makes the manuscript evidence for the New Testament so impressive? How does this affect the English translations we have today?

4. What are the points of external evidence that indicate verses 9–20 were not part of Mark's gospel? What points of internal evidence indicate the same?

5. Why does Mark end the way he does, in 16:8? What theme has Mark been developing throughout his gospel? In light of that theme, how is this seeming non-ending actually a strong conclusion to Mark's gospel?

6. Why is there so much Christless preaching in the modern church? How does knowing Christ from the New Testament help us see Him in the Old Testament?

PONDERING THE PRINCIPLES

1. As with the opening of this sermon, Charles Spurgeon memorably also affirmed the Bible's ability to defend itself as he preached it.

> There seems to me to have been twice as much done in some ages in defending the Bible as in expounding it, but if the whole of our strength shall henceforth go to the exposition and spreading of it, we may leave it pretty much to defend itself. I do not know whether you see that lion—it is very distinctly before my eyes; a number of persons advance to attack him, while a host of us would defend the grand old monarch .... Pardon me if I offer a quiet suggestion. Open the door and let the lion out; he will take care of himself. ("The Bible—2," *Speeches by C. H. Spurgeon, at Home and Abroad*, ed. G. H. Pike [London: Passmore & Alabaster, 1878], 17)

The more you study Scripture, the more it demonstrates its truthfulness and power. In fact, the gospel revealed in the Bible is the power of God for salvation (Rom. 1:16). It is the Word that accomplishes God's work (Isa. 55:10–11; Jas. 1:18; 1 Pet. 1:23). Think about how you normally answer questions and objections concerning the truth of Scripture. Are you more prone to get in front of the lion or to let it out of the cage?

2. Mark's gospel is all about "The Amazing Jesus." Throughout the book, people are repeatedly amazed, astonished, and even frightened by Jesus and His works. All of this culminates with Mark's conclusion—everyone is left speechless. Is that your response when you read about Christ? Or has your heart become dull toward the Lord? Believers ought to be gripped with amazement and love for their Lord. Spend some time reading the gospel of Mark, taking note of specific instances where His remarkable words and works are displayed.

THE TALE OF TWO SONS

INTRODUCTION

The text before us, like so many texts, is very familiar. Yet it contains many surprising elements, and that's the genius of our Lord as a teacher. Some, including literary giants Charles Dickens and Ralph Waldo Emerson, have called the parable of the prodigal son the greatest short story ever written. That may make you think, "What am I missing? Is there something in this story I haven't seen?" And there is.

A. The Aim of Salvation

1. God's glory

To introduce the story, I want to remind you of some of Jonathan Edwards's Resolutions:

a. Number one: "Resolved, that I will do whatsoever I think to be most to God's glory."

b. Number four: "Resolved, never to do any manner of thing, whether in soul or body, less or more, but what tends to the glory of God."

c. Number twenty-three: "Resolved, frequently to take some deliberate action . . . for the glory of God . . . and if I find it not to be for God's glory, to repute it as a breach of the fourth Resolution."

d. Number twenty-seven: "Resolved, never willfully to omit anything, except the omission be for the glory of God; and frequently to examine my omissions."

2. God's joy

Jonathan Edwards was consumed with the glory of God. And he understood that God was too. Edwards said that God infinitely values His own glory. In fact, His infinite joy consists in His infinite glory.

3. God's redemptive work

In history, the glory of God is nowhere displayed like it is in the salvation of sinners. Edwards wrote, "God has greatly glorified himself in the work of creation and providence. All his works praise him, and his glory shines brightly from them all: but as some stars differ from others in glory, so the glory of God shines brighter in some of his works than in others. And amongst all these, the work of redemption is like the sun in his strength. The glory of the author is abundantly the most resplendent in this work" (Jonathan Edwards, "The Wisdom of God Displayed in the Way of Salvation" in *The Works of Jonathan Edwards*, vol. 2 [Edinburgh: The Banner of Truth Trust, 1974], 144).

Edwards believed that the glory of Christ's redemptive work to obtain His bride surpassed even His work of creation. In fact, God's purpose in redemption was a *unique* display of His glory, and thus, of His joy in saving sinners. We see that depicted in this parable.

B. The Followers of Christ

In the last verse of the previous chapter, Jesus said, "He who has ears to hear, let him hear" (Luke 14:35). That is a call to those who are willing to listen to His message of salvation. Luke 15:1 tells us who was listening: "Now all the tax collectors and the sinners were coming near Him to listen to Him." It was the outcasts—the scum, the riffraff, the lowlifes—who were listening, believing, and being saved.

Those two categories—tax collectors and sinners—described the worst of the worst.

1. Tax collectors were the lowest people in Israel, socially and religiously.

   Rome, which occupied Israel at the time, sold tax franchises, and certain Jews would buy them—greedy men who did not care about their own people or their religion and looked to capitalize on the pagan occupation of their own nation. They strong-armed the people for their money, taking what Rome required plus whatever more they could extort. These "businesses" essentially became a criminal operation, like the mafia.

   Tax collectors were surrounded by thugs who helped extract the money from taxpayers. They were unsynagogued, estranged from society, and put out of families. They were considered outside God's purposes. They were the traitors of all traitors, hated by the people.

2. The term "sinners" includes the thugs that usually surrounded tax collectors, as well as the lowlife criminals and prostitutes who carried out base, immoral activity in Israel.

The rabbis said that no one should associate with such people, not even to bring them near to the law of God. But they were the ones who came to Jesus and listened.

C. The Opponents of Christ

Verse 2 says, "Both the Pharisees and the scribes began to grumble, saying, 'This man receives sinners and eats with them.'"

1. Religious regulators

The Pharisees and scribes were the religious elite. They worked hand in hand, the scribes as textual experts informing the religion of the Pharisees. Together, they plied their legalistic religion through the local synagogues, and had the ears of the people as a result. They were in every town and village and neighborhood through their control of the synagogue. They dominated life in Israel.

2. Self-righteous snobs

These religious leaders were self-righteous. They believed that you earned your way into God's kingdom by external morality and observing the required ceremonies. They were the "in" people. They were the pure—far too pure to be polluted by any association with sinners. So when they saw Jesus associating with sinners, they drew one conclusion: He is of Satan because He associates with Satan's people.

These self-appointed, self-righteous "holy" men looked down on Jesus with malice. They assigned Him a place with Satan and the kingdom of darkness, claiming He did His works by Satan's power (cf. Matt. 9:34; Mark 3:22; Luke 11:15).

Jesus was doing God's work—the work of redeeming sinners—in which God is glorified and has great joy. But the Jewish leaders saw it as the work of Satan. They were so far from God that they were opposed to His central work.

D. The Parables of Christ

Jesus' response to their self-righteous, anti-evangelistic attitude was to reveal their distance from God—to show them they knew nothing of His glory and joy. He did so with three stories.

1. A lost sheep (vv. 3–7)

The first is about a man who pursues one lost sheep out of a flock of one hundred. The man goes out, finds the sheep, and rejoices with his friends because he values the sheep (vv. 4–6). The Lord concludes, "I tell you that in the same way, there will be more joy in heaven over one sinner who repents than over ninety-nine righteous persons who need no repentance" (v. 7).

Heaven rejoices over one sinner's repentance. But the religious leaders didn't understand that.

2. A lost coin (vv. 8–10)

The second story was about a woman who lost

a coin—like in the first story, this is a valuable object. But she finds the coin and calls her friends together, saying, "Rejoice with me, for I have found the coin which I had lost!" (v. 9). Then Jesus reveals the lesson: "In the same way, I tell you, there is joy in the presence of the angels of God over one sinner who repents" (v. 10).

The point is that the Jewish leaders were so far from God, and so different from Him. God's joy was in the salvation of one sinner—but they couldn't understand that.

Heaven is not waiting for ten thousand sinners— or one thousand, or one hundred, or even ten—to repent in order to start celebrating. God has joy in the salvation of a solitary sinner. That is Jesus' point in this chapter.

LESSON

The context for Jesus' final parable in Luke 15 was Middle Eastern village peasant life—very foreign to our own context, for the most part. And one particular feature of that culture sheds light on the story's meaning: the shame-honor paradigm. Everything in that setting was viewed through the grid of what was honorable and what was shameful.

People in that context had a clear understanding of shame and honor—it was practically ingrained into their subconscious. And even more so for the Pharisees and scribes. Shame and honor were crucial to them, as it always is to hypocrites.

In such a context, Jesus' parable was incomprehensible. It was a ridiculous barrage of shame, inconceivable to the minds of His listeners. Every aspect of the story was counterintuitive and ran against the grain of their society. The Pharisees would have walked away shaking their heads and rolling their eyes. The story was shameful from start to finish.

I. A SHAMEFUL REQUEST (LUKE 15:11–12)

This is not a story about a son; it's a story about *a man* who had *two* sons (v. 11). "The younger of them said to his father, 'Father, give me the share of the estate that falls to me'" (v. 12).

A. The Son's Audacity

While the younger son addresses his father respectfully, the request he makes is unthinkable. The *younger* son is asking the father for his share of an inheritance. But he's out of rank. There's a pecking order: The older should receive his inheritance first.

B. The Son's Selfishness

Worse than that, this is extraordinary selfishness. The estate would fall to the sons when the father died, so this is like saying, "Father, I wish you were dead. I want what's mine, and I want it now. You're in the way of that." He sees the father as an impediment, a restraint—an unwelcome point of accountability. The son wants freedom, independence. And he wants his father's money.

C. The Son's Disdain

This disrespectful request was a blatant violation of the commandment to honor your parents (Ex. 20:12). The young man wasn't interested in his family relationships.

D. The Son's Greed

The son says, "Give me the share of the estate" (Gk., *tēs ousias*), that is, the father's property and goods. He doesn't want his inheritance so he can develop and use it for the family's good; he wants the cash. He isn't asking so that he can take over the management of what would be his in the future. He wants nothing to do with the family.

There was no precedent in Jewish society for this. It is an outrageous, shameful request. Those listening, especially the Pharisees, would expect one thing: The father would raise his right hand and slap that young man in the face. And then he would punish him severely, beating him publicly, because the father had to protect his honor at all costs.

II. A SHAMEFUL RESPONSE (LUKE 15:12)

"So he divided his wealth between them."

The father does not protect his honor. He does exactly what this willful, hateful son asks.

A. Dishonorable Compliance

It was absurd. The estate was to be apportioned to the sons—two thirds to the older and one third to the younger—*only after* the father died. Maybe a father would do it early for some noble cause, but certainly not to fund the rebellion of a disrespectful son.

We would expect the father to do everything to protect his own honor. He's been publicly embarrassed by this son, and now he needs to take the high ground and preserve his honor. But he does the exact opposite. He acts in this shameful way, making himself a dishonorable, ridiculous father.

So first, no son should ever have made this request. Second, no father should ever have granted it. The whole situation is an outrage.

B. Dishonorable Love

Someone might say, "The father must really love the boy." But it's a kind of love that seems foolish. It certainly isn't tough love. It's ridiculous to give the boy his freedom, letting him go do as he will, when the father knows what the boy is like. A loving parent would do everything he could to pull the boy in tighter.

C. Dishonorable Family

Interestingly, the older son had the responsibility of protecting the father's honor and protecting younger siblings from foolishness. But the older son does not appear at this point in the story. Perhaps some of the listeners were saying, "Where was the older brother? Why wasn't he fulfilling his duty to preserve the father's honor? Why didn't he stop his younger brother from doing something foolish?" So even the older brother bears some of the shame in this story.

III. A SHAMEFUL REBELLION (LUKE 15:13–16)

The father divided the estate, which means the older son received his two thirds, and the younger son received his one third. That launches the shameful rebellion. Verse 13 says, "And not many days later," to indicate how fast this young man acts. He is driven by passion and evil desire, so there's no delay—he moves as fast as he can.

A. Liquidating the Estate (v. 13)

"...the younger son gathered everything together..."

That expression means he turned his share into cash. The father's estate had been accumulating for generations in the family. It was evidently very large because there were servants, hired men, musicians, a fatted calf—all of that demonstrates significant wealth. To rapidly liquidate an estate like that requires selling below market value. The young man trivializes his family's inheritance and sells it at a discount for fast cash.

In Jewish culture, such a purchase wasn't immediately redeemable; it was a futures purchase. The buyer wouldn't receive the younger son's inheritance until the father died, but was still willing to purchase it because of the discount. So the son turns the property over to a stranger for quick cash.

This is stupid—sacrificing your future on the altar of the immediate.

B. Escaping the Family (v. 13)

"… and went on a journey into a distant country …"

He gets as far away from home as he can—away from all accountability and restraint. That way he can live however he wants without his family knowing.

At this point, there would have been a funeral. That's why the father says later in verse 24, "This son of mine was dead"—he is dead to the family.

C. Wasting the Inheritance (v. 13)

"... and there he squandered his estate with loose living."

Driven by lust, the son wastes everything. That is why he is called the *prodigal* son—it's a term that means "wasteful." He spends down his future and then has nothing to show for it but dissipated, debauched, irresponsible living. Later on in the story, his older brother points out that he wasted much of it on prostitutes (v. 30).

D. Facing the Famine (vv. 14–15)

"Now when he had spent everything, a severe famine occurred in that country, and he began to be impoverished. So he went and hired himself out to [or attached himself to] one of the citizens of that county ..."

His debauchery was his fault, but some things weren't. Famine brings people very low. Historically, it has driven people to eat garbage, sandals, stray animals, and other disgusting things, like Israel did while starving under siege (cf. 2 Kings 6:24–29). It is miserable.

So the younger son becomes a beggar. And the word translated "hired himself out" (Gk., *kollaō*) means "to glue." That's what beggars do. Perhaps you've experienced this in your own travels—they follow you, stick their hands in your pockets, and pull on your clothes in hopes of getting something.

E. Feeding the Swine (v. 15)

"... and he sent him into his fields to feed swine."

So this prodigal finds a citizen in this far-off Gentile country and glues himself to him, and eventually the citizen sends him into the field to feed swine. It wasn't a legitimate hire; the boy may have thought it was, but it was just a way to get rid of this relentless beggar.

You can understand the outrage. The shame of the younger son's demand to the father, the shame of the father's funding his rebellion, the shame of selling the estate cheap for fast cash, the shame of funding gross, immoral living, the shame of becoming a beggar attached to a Gentile, and now the shame of being sent to feed pigs. The crowds probably rolled their eyes and said, "No Jewish boy would do that. This could never happen."

F. Reaching the Pits (v. 16)

"And he would have gladly filled his stomach with the pods that the swine were eating, and no one was giving anything to him."

It gets worse. He's ostensibly out there to feed the pigs, he went out thinking he had a job, but no one gives him anything to survive on. So now, he has to fight the pigs for the carob pods they eat. He's gone from prosperity to sticking his face between the pig snouts to get a share of their food in a Gentile land.

The shame is beyond comprehension.

G. Nearing the End (v. 17)

"... I am dying here with hunger!"

The boy is starving. He can't beat the pigs to the pods. He is beyond desperate.

Jesus was using this to describe the desperation of the sinner—poor, destitute, hungry, hopeless, debauched, and dying. This is desperation.

1. Sin as rebellion

   Jesus' lesson was that sin is rebellion against God. And God gives people the freedom to sin and to take it as far as they choose.

2. Sin as disdain

   This parable shows the rebellion of a man who had no relationship to the one who gave him life. He had no relationship to the one who held all the riches he could ever need. He had no relationship to the one who held his future as well as his present. That's how it is with sin; sin is disdain for God and His rule, authority, will, goodness, and resources.

3. Sin as evasion

   Sin is a desire to run from God and to avoid all accountability to Him. It is to deny God any place in your life. It is to dishonor Him and to take all the loving gifts He gives and squander them as far away from Him as you can get.

4. Sin as dissipation

Sin is wasteful, self-indulgent dissipation and unrestrained lust. It is shunning all God's goodness. It is reckless evil that takes you to the brink of death. Sin looks for fulfillment away from God and never finds it. It leaves the sinner exhausted, empty, hungry, and hopeless.

The picture is extreme. But the question is: How is the father going to deal with a sinner like this? Jesus has invented the ultimate sinner. This son is the epitome of shame: He is guilty of disrespect to parents, disrespect to community, dissipation of his own body, unbounded immorality, violation of all cultural constraints. And now, he lives in a despised place with a despised people. This is not skid row; the skid is over. This is rock bottom.

IV. A SHAMEFUL REPENTANCE
(LUKE 15:17–20a)

But the shame is not over. A shameful repentance follows.

A. Coming to His Senses (v. 17)

"But when he came to his senses, he said, 'How many of my father's hired men have more than enough bread, but I am dying here with hunger!'"

That's always the start of repentance. You begin to assess your true condition and realize the sorry state you're in.

B. Remembering His Father (v. 17)

1. Lowly workers

The social structure of a village like this was topped by wealthy landowners, then tenant farmers, then small business owners, craftsman, and so on. Then there were the servants. A family would hire a servant, house him, and feed him— the servant basically became part of the family. There were also "hired men" (Gk., *misthios*), day laborers who made themselves available in public places in hopes of being hired for the day. They were dependent on that daily wage (cf. Lev. 19:13; Matt. 20:1–16).

2. Generous father

Hired men were low in the social order, doing mostly unskilled, menial work. But the son says that his father's hired men have "more than enough." That tells us the father was generous, even with the people who were at the bottom of the economic ladder. Such people would normally just eke out an existence, but not in the employ of this father. He is merciful and good.

This is where the young man begins to realize the goodness of his father. His father gave more than enough to his hired men, but the son is dying from hunger. So he begins to trust in his father's goodness and love. Where he once scorned that mercy, now he recalls and begins to trust in it.

C. Relying on His Father's Character (vv. 18–19)

"I will get up and go to my father, and will say to him, 'Father, I have sinned against heaven, and in your sight; I am no longer worthy to be called your son; make me as one of your hired men.'"

He's thinking, "I'm going to trust my father's mercy. The way he treats the lowest people proves that somehow, he will receive me. I know his compassionate nature."

D. Knowing His Shame (vv. 18–19)

This is embarrassing. He not only has to face his father, but his older brother and the whole village. The father has been publicly shamed, but so has the son, and the community will ridicule and disdain him. That was part of the cultural punishment, to uphold the honor of the father and the village.

E. Anticipating His Servitude (v. 19)

Not only that, but the son would face a future of hard labor. That is the only way he could begin to make restitution for the third of the estate he squandered. It would take years and years to pay his father back—and only once the restitution was complete would there be any hope of reconciliation.

F. Considering His Confession (v. 18)

The boy admits in verse 18, "I have sinned against heaven." Even in practicing his petition in his mind, he does not ask for privileges or attempt to claim rights—he knows he has forfeited them all. He will not ask to live in the house or to be part of the family again. He will not even ask to be a servant. All he wants is for the father to show him enough mercy to let him work as a day laborer on minimum wage. Then, maybe, he can eventually earn back what he lost and attain reconciliation with his father.

He realizes his options away from his father are exhausted, and all they have brought is death. He will pay any price for the life his father has—the punishment, the humiliation, the hard labor—he is desperate. That is the picture of a sinner in true repentance, realizing his path leads to death. He desires reconciliation and is willing to confess his sins to get it—he's willing to do anything.

At this point, the Pharisees and scribes would have been saying to themselves, "That's exactly what that boy should do"; this is the first thing that made any sense to them.

Well, he did.

G. Returning to the Father (v. 20)

"So he got up and came to his father."

He gets up and goes to his father, filthy and stinking, trudging toward the village.

1. The proper reception

The Pharisees also knew what the father should do once the son came back. The father's opportunity to restore his honor had arrived—he should remain in his house, and when someone brings the news that his younger son has returned, he should say, "Let him sit in his putrid clothes and endure the scorn and mockery of the village. And then, after four days, I will see him."

2. The proper restitution

The father would expect him to come in, bow down, kiss his feet, and receive the due punishment—perhaps a lashing. Then it was time to begin the work he would do—for decades. If he could continue in that work for long enough, then maybe reconciliation would be possible. But only after restitution was made. As the rabbis said, there is no reconciliation without restitution.

But none of the shameful behavior in the story so far amounts to what comes next.

V. A SHAMEFUL RECONCILIATION
(LUKE 15:20*b*–21)

"But while [the young man] was still a long way off, his

father saw him and felt compassion for him, and ran and embraced him and kissed him."

The son is still outside the village, walking the dusty road, perhaps toward a gate or the perimeter of the town. Yet while he is still far away, his father sees him, feels compassion for him, runs, embraces, and kisses him. The father is making himself a bigger fool than the son.

A. The Seeking Father (v. 20)

"But while he was still a long way off, his father saw him . . ."

The father must have been looking out for the son. And we can assume it was the father's habit, since he is doing it on this occasion. The father is the seeker.

B. The Compassionate Father (v. 20)

". . . and felt compassion for him . . ."

This would only make the man weaker, in the eyes of the Pharisees.

C. The Ignominious Father (v. 20)

". . . and ran . . ."

1. Running

It gets worse—the father starts running. This was unthinkable for Middle Eastern noblemen. Not because they weren't capable of running, but because it, too, was dishonorable. There is an entire body of Jewish literature written about the fact that men shouldn't run.

2. Lifting

Men wore robes that covered their legs because it was considered shameful for them to be visible. But to run in such a robe required you to lift it and uncover your legs. That was so unacceptable that Jewish literature said priests could not even lift their robe to keep it out of the blood while offering sacrifices. One rabbi condemned a man for lifting his robe above his knees to keep it from getting caught in some thorn bushes (Kenneth E. Bailey, *Finding the Lost: Cultural Keys to Luke 15* [St. Louis: Concordia Publishing House, 1992], 145).

A man was not supposed to run. First, because it wasn't dignified; they were supposed to carry themselves in a stately manner. Second, it was shameful to show your lower body.

3. Sprinting

The word "ran" (Gk., *trechō*) in verse 20 could be used of someone sprinting in a race. This man rushes out of his house and sprints through the middle of town toward this son, while the onlookers are appalled. This is an indecent, shameful thing. The rabbis said a man should not even jump, for fear somebody might see his lower leg. In fact, robes were called *mkbdut*, which means "that which gives me honor" (Bailey, *Finding the Lost*, 145).

D. The Self-Sacrificing Father (v. 20)

The father is running through town, bringing shame on himself, in a selfless act of condescension. Why? Because he wants to get to the son before the son arrives—as soon as the son enters the village, he will be mocked, scorned, and ridiculed. But the father takes the shame, in order to get to his son first. This is truly shocking behavior for a Middle Eastern nobleman.

E. The Reconciling Father (v. 20)

". . . and embraced him and kissed him."

When the father reaches the pig-scented rebel, he embraces him and kisses him on the head. This is full reconciliation. He does not shame the boy—he takes the shame instead. And everyone knows that he has received the boy fully as a son.

F. The Gracious Father (v. 21)

"And the son said to him, 'Father, I have sinned against heaven and in your sight; I am no longer worthy to be called your son.'"

The son should have been beaten. He should have been forced to sit in the open and take the shame. That's what the villagers would have thought.

One word describes all of this: *grace*. But the Jewish religious leaders didn't understand grace.

1. An adjusted confession

   Notice the son stops short. He leaves out part of the speech he'd rehearsed. In verse 19 he'd included, "Make me as one of your hired men." He'd planned to say it, but he doesn't once his father embraces him—*because he knows he doesn't have to earn back his father's love*. He doesn't have to earn reconciliation. He receives grace.

   It would have been an insult to his father's compassion if he had continued his speech. So he simply repents and entrusts himself to his father's mercy. That is all that's required of any sinner in need of salvation.

2. An outrageous attribute

   Grace, of course, outraged the Pharisees continuously. They were repulsed by Jesus embracing sinners and granting them reconciliation. But Jesus depicted this young man as receiving forgiveness and sonship, and all he did was turn from his sin and trust in his father.

G. The Ultimate Father

The father in this parable is really God the Son, coming down from heaven to the dust of our towns to seek and save the lost sinner. *God initiates salvation*—He is the seeker. God sees the sinner before the sinner sees Him, and He runs the gauntlet and takes their shame. His love is lavish, His grace is limitless, and He delights in the salvation of one lost sinner.

We have a lot of thoughts about God, but that's not normally one of them. We're not used to thinking of God as so effusive, lavish, and loving to the worst sinner. But this prodigal son got it—he was reconciled.

To the Pharisees, this was a shameful reconciliation. They thought the father was in breach of justice, righteousness, and honor. They never understood God's love for sinners, let alone His condescending to our level and suffering on our behalf.

VI. A SHAMEFUL REJOICING (LUKE 15:22–24)

A. An Instantaneous Salvation (v. 22)

"But the father said to his slaves, 'Quickly . . .'"

Salvation happens in an instant. It is not a long process of restoration by works and ceremony. "*Quickly*"—the father immediately reinstates for the prodigal, on the spot, all the privileges of being his son.

B. A Lavish Salvation (v. 22)

1. Dignity restored

"... bring out the best robe and put it on him ..."

This would have been the father's own robe, used only on the most special occasions. It would have been a beautifully embroidered robe, possibly a family heirloom worn by the father and his father before him.

He doesn't say to the young man, "Go and get yourself cleaned up." He treats him like a king. He calls all the servants and tells them to put the robe on his son while he simply stands there.

It was a robe of dignity. The prodigal now shares the dignity of his father.

2. Authority restored

"... and put a ring on his hand ..."

This wasn't just for looks—it bore the family symbol, which could be pressed in soft wax to seal official documents. It signifies authority to act on behalf of the father. It's like getting the keys to the kingdom.

3. Responsibility restored

"... and sandals on his feet ..."

Slaves and hired men didn't wear shoes; they were for people with responsibility.

So he is given the father's dignity, authority, and responsibility. This is full sonship.

How grace triumphs over sin! Grace gives us the dignity of Christ as we are clothed with His own righteousness, the authority of Christ to act as His ambassadors consistent with His revelation, and the responsibility to carry on His work in His name and in the power of His Spirit.

C. A Joyous Salvation (vv. 23–24)

". . . and bring the fattened calf, kill it, and let us eat and celebrate . . ."

1. A reason for rejoicing (v. 23)

   Wealthy people usually kept one calf for their biggest and best occasion, like the marriage of an eldest son. They would kill the calf and cut it into steaks and chops to cook in their ovens. It is time to celebrate.

   Earlier, in verse 7, Jesus said, "There will be more joy in heaven over one sinner who repents than over ninety-nine righteous persons who need no repentance." Verse 10 says, "There is joy in the presence of the angels of God over one sinner who repents." That is exactly what happens here, upon the prodigal's return.

2. A host worthy of honor (v. 23)

   One important point to note is that the celebration is directed toward *the father*, not the son. The son receives the robe, ring, and shoes, but the party is in honor of *such a gracious father*.

3. An event for everyone (v. 23)

> A calf could feed anywhere from a hundred to two hundred people—this is a big celebration. And in such societies, people didn't eat meat very often—it was for special occasions. So this is a very special event.

4. A rescue and restoration (v. 24)

> ". . . for this son of mine was dead and has come to life again; he was lost and has been found."

> God knows who His sons are—they are His by sovereign election. And He has fixed the time when, in His wonderful providence, He will raise each one from death to life.

5. A celebration of grace (v. 24)

> "And they began to celebrate."

> So they begin the celebration that will never end—the celebration over the redemption of every sinner. And it is a celebration of God—the extravagantly gracious, saving God.

This turn in the plot is another outrage to the listening Pharisees and scribes. It is no longer just bizarre; it is provoking, like fingernails down a blackboard. The father acts shamefully and stupidly, giving all of this to the son and then celebrating as if he deserved honor.

They didn't have a character like this in their world—there weren't sons like this, and there weren't fathers like this. And that is their unmasking. *They did not know God.*

VII. A SHAMEFUL REACTION (LUKE 15:25–28*a*)

A. Estranged from the Father (v. 25)

"Now his older son was in the field, and when he came and approached the house . . ."

Jesus continued the story toward its conclusion. You would expect the older son to be involved in planning a big event like this; that is his responsibility. But the father never consults him or even tells him about it—why? *Because he has no relationship with the father either.* The older son, like his younger brother, hates and is alienated from his father. He's just stayed around rather than running off.

B. Indifferent to the Father (v. 25)

That's why the older son doesn't defend his father's honor at the beginning of the story. That's why he doesn't try to protect his brother from his folly. Although he lives at the house, this young man has no relationship with his father. The father knows he doesn't care about his brother or about his father's joy. So the older son isn't invited to the party.

He was out in the field—not working, himself, but making sure everyone else was. When he arrives home at the usual time, the party has already started.

C. Alienated from the Father (vv. 25–27)

"... when he came and approached the house, he heard music and dancing. And he summoned one of the servants and began inquiring what these things could be. And he said to him, 'Your brother has come, and your father has killed the fattened calf because he has received him back safe and sound.'"

The Greek word translated "servants" could refer to the village boys who are outside while the adults are in the house having the party. And the elder son is totally in the dark about what has transpired. He's played no part in the redemptive scheme. So one of the boys has to fill him in.

The phrase "safe and sound" is connected to the Hebrew word *shalom*—the younger son is now at peace with his father. He's received full reconciliation.

D. Angry at the Father (v. 28)

1. Enraged

"But he became angry ..."

You might think the older son would celebrate the reconciliation. But no, he becomes angry.

This is the Pharisees and scribes. They were angry that God in Christ was embracing sinners. Earlier, they were the ninety-nine sheep who needed no repentance because they didn't see themselves as sinners (v. 4); here, they are the older brother.

2. Unwilling

> "... and was not willing to go in ..."
>
> He wants no part of this. His father is shameful. His younger brother is shameful, and the villagers who celebrate are shameful. To him, this is no time to honor his father—his father is a fool.

The older son has been at home all those years, but he has no relationship with his father. He is as lost as his brother was. He is the perfect picture of the Pharisees and scribes, who were just as lost as the tax collectors and sinners—they were just a different kind of lost. Some are lost in a far country; some are lost at home. Some are lost in the world; some are lost in the church.

Truth be told, legalists and superficially religious people, like this older brother, are jealous of prodigals because they have the same lusts but never fulfill them. They have the same hankering for iniquity, so they are envious of those who play out their lusts without a care for what others think; they are constrained because their approach to get what they want is to conform outwardly to religious requirements.

But the Pharisees would have seen this older brother and said, "Finally, a sensible man. He understands." This was their kind of guy—because this was them.

VIII. A SHAMEFUL REPLY (LUKE 15:28*b*–32)

". . . and his father came out and began pleading with him."

The shame continues with the father's reply to the older son at the end of verse 28. It's unbelievable. The father condescends once again, leaving the celebration where he is the guest of honor, going out into the darkening field, finding this hypocrite who hates him, and begging him to come to the party.

This is another disgraceful act. Again, the father does not punish a son for insulting him. There is no public slap, no public punishment. Instead, the father entreats his son to join them.

A. Another Spiteful Son (v. 29)

"But he answered and said to his father, 'Look!'"

This was no way to address a father. He should say, "Father, Father," not, "Look!" That is disdain and disrespect. It's the older son's way of saying, "I wish you were dead," as the younger son had done at the outset.

B. Another Begrudging Son (v. 29)

"Look! For so many years I have been serving you and I have never neglected a command of yours . . ."

That's how it is with legalists. They conform because of duty—and it's a bitter grind. The older son has deceived himself into thinking that he has kept the law, much like the rich young ruler in Luke 18:18–23. That is the way of religious phonies and hypocrites—they won't admit their sin.

C. Another Selfish Son (vv. 29–30)

". . . and yet you have never given me a young goat, so that I might celebrate with my friends; but when this son of yours came, who has devoured your wealth with prostitutes, you killed the fattened calf for him."

The older son has been grinding away, serving the father—in order to get the estate he wants. And he is resentful. He wants a party of his own, not with his father or his brother. He has his own group of friends—fellow hypocrites he'd rather be with.

D. Another Beloved Son (vv. 31–32)

"And he said to him, 'Son, you have always been with me, and all that is mine is yours. But we had to celebrate and rejoice, for this brother of yours was dead and has begun to live, and was lost and has been found.'"

The father responds by calling him "Child," using the Greek word *teknon* rather than *huios* ("son"), which appears eight times in this passage. This was an affectionate address despite the son's tantrum— "My child" or "My boy." The father tells him that he would have gladly given him everything if the son had sought a relationship with him—the father has been right there. Those things were not to be earned through reluctant, resentful labor.

The Pharisees, despite agreeing with the older son's perspective, couldn't understand how the father could endure appearing this weak. How could he not strike such a shameful son? But the father's focus, verse 32 shows, was on rejoicing because a son who had been dead had been restored to him. "We *had to* celebrate" (emphasis added).

Jesus shows us two kinds of sinners in this story: the debauched, irreligious profligate, and the religious hypocrite in the house. One distant from the church and openly immoral, the other around the church and externally pure. And He shows us the father who entreats them both, who offers both everything he has.

The point is that even the extreme sinner falls within the purview of God's grace, and so does everyone in between. The Lord rejoices in the repentance of one sinner, with all the holy angels and glorified saints.

CONCLUSION

When the story ends in verse 32, you look for verse 33 because it doesn't feel complete. What happened next? How did the older son respond?

A. The Ending Written

If we were to write an ending, here is how it might go: "The older brother, seeing the mercy of his father and his desire for reconciliation, confessed his sin and hypocrisy and asked his father for forgiveness. The father embraced him, kissed him, took him into the banquet, and seated him at his table." I like that ending. But we can't write the ending—it's already been written.

This is the ending: "Upon hearing this, the older son, outraged at his father, picked up a piece of wood and beat him to death."

B. The Ending Realized

It would be only a few months before the Pharisees killed Jesus by nailing Him on a wooden cross. And they would congratulate themselves for recovering the honor of their people, nation, and religion from one who covered it in shame.

In the imagery of this parable, that would be the son striking the father with crushing blows while saying, "You are evil and shameful! Someone needs to end the shame and bring honor to this family—and I will do it by ridding us of such a shameful father." And he states this while beating his father to death.

That's how the story ended, and the final irony is that the father who should have beaten the son is beaten to death by him instead, in the greatest act of evil ever.

The religious elites thought they were righteous, but they didn't understand love, mercy, and grace. Yet God, the saving, gracious Father in Christ, used that murder as the means by which He purchased our salvation. It all ended at the cross where Christ endured death, despising the shame for us (Heb. 12:2). He took the shame so that you could be at the celebration of His joy.

FOCUSING ON THE FACTS

1. What was the context in which Jesus told this parable? How does that context help us understand the parable's meaning? Consider both the immediate context in Christ's ministry as well as the wider cultural context of a shame-honor society.

2. What is Jesus teaching, through the actions of the prodigal son, about the nature of sin? Can you identify those same attitudes or deeds in your own life—and the lives of others? What can you conclude about God's perspective on sin through seeing it depicted by the prodigal son's rebellion against his gracious father?

3. What does this story teach about the nature of repentance? How does understanding the nature of God fuel repentance and motivate us to seek forgiveness when we sin?

4. What is the main point Christ is making about Himself in this story? What does that teach us about God? How do the shameful actions of the father in the parable reflect the Son of God's condescension to save sinners?

5. Do you think of God as delighting in the salvation of sinners? Why is it important that we remind ourselves of that truth?

6. How was the older son different from his younger brother? How were they similar? Who was more lost? What does this say about the Pharisees, and the self-righteous religious people of today?

7. What does the father's response to the older son's complaints reveal about the father's heart toward him?

8. Why was the character of the father so repulsive to the Pharisees? What did their attitude toward him reveal about their attitude toward Christ and God? Why did the Pharisees have such a hard time understanding grace? Why do people today have that same problem?

PONDERING THE PRINCIPLES

1. Sometimes when we think about sin, we remove it from the context of our relationship to God. We rightly think of sin as violating a righteous standard, but we miss that it is offending our God—Father, Son, and Holy Spirit. It is insulting and rejecting the one who gave us life and every good gift we enjoy. It is exchanging the Creator for the creation. It is wanting our Father's blessings, but hating Him. It is telling God that we wish He were dead. It is fleeing as far away as possible from Him. Yet God still shows repentant sinners mercy.

   That perspective on sin ought to make us ever more grateful for God's grace in saving us and ever more cautious of sin. Especially as believers, we do not want to violate our relationship with our loving father. Do you tend to take sin in your life this seriously, or do you usually dismiss or overlook its importance? Take time to consider carefully, confess your sins, seek the Lord's forgiveness, and praise Him for His grace.

2. This parable makes tangible the difference between Christ and the Pharisees. The religious elite of God's chosen people, who claimed to know God and to speak for Him, were exposed as His enemies on one crucial point—their response to sinners. The story of the prodigal son shows that the Lord loves, seeks, condescends, and sacrifices for sinners. He receives and restores them. He, and all heaven with Him, rejoices in

their salvation. The Pharisees despised, scorned, and separated from lost sinners. They hated when Jesus showed sinners mercy. To Israel's spiritual leaders, the wicked were merely a foil to make their own superficial righteousness a little more convincing.

Whom do you identify with most? Do you share the compassion for sinners that Christ had? Do you find joy in their salvation? Or do you find yourself shaking your head with the Pharisees and scoffing at the idea that such a one could be freely restored by God's grace?

3. In the older son's rude reply to his father's pleas, he spoke of "this son of yours" (v. 30), distancing himself from his shameful brother. But as the compassionate father replied to his bitter older son, he called his younger son "this brother of yours" (v. 32)—closing the gap between them. As we saw, the two sons were essentially the same—internally, they were both rebellious sinners in need of their father's grace.

Too often, professing believers have an ungracious attitude toward wayward sinners—we look down our noses at them as if they were substantively different to ourselves. When we do that, we prove we don't understand—or appreciate—God's grace. We must strive to purge ourselves of that kind of hypocrisy by recovering the truth of God's lavish grace toward us in Christ. Reflect on how the father in this parable deals with his sons and how that reveals the grace of God. Read Psalm 103, and consider how God's love is displayed there.

4. It is remarkable how kindly the father deals with his older son. He pleaded with him to come into the house despite his hard-heartedness (v. 28). He met his contemptuous words with compassionate grace: "Son . . . all that is mine is yours" (v. 31). He was still willing to receive his son, if the son would only receive his grace. Perhaps this passage has brought you to recognize your own guilt, which you have been masking in self-righteousness. Amazingly, the Lord will still receive you if you would only confess your sins, repent of them, and trust in His mercy.